How to keep away from the psychiatrist

...

by Jack MacArthur

Tyndale House Publishers, Inc.
Wheaton, Illinois

Coverdale House Publishers, Ltd.
London, England

How to Keep Away from the Psychiatrist, previously published by Certain Sound Publishing House, a division of Vernon L. Iverson Co., under the title *Short Beds, Narrow Covers.* All rights assigned to Tyndale House Publishers, Inc. ◆ Library of Congress Catalog Card Number 74-15436. ISBN 8423-1516-0, paper. Copyright © 1974 Tyndale House Publishers, Inc., Wheaton, Illinois. All rights reserved. First printing, July 1975. Printed in the United States of America.

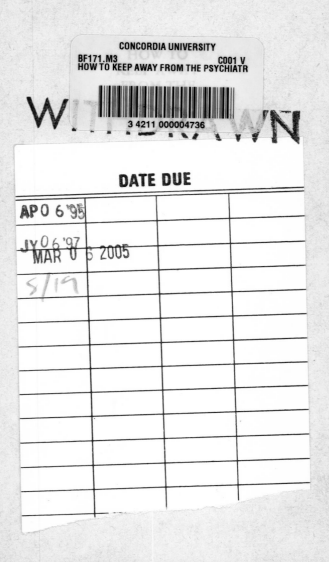

DATE DUE

AP 0 6 '95			
JY 06 '97			
MAR 0 6 2005			
5/19			

In dedication and gratitude to my friend

Lee Hoskinson

who insisted this humble effort be put into print
and whose devotion and selfless service
for our Lord Jesus Christ
has been a special source of inspiration to me.

All Scripture quotations
are taken from *The Living Bible*
unless indicated otherwise.

† = various paraphrases combined for clarity

CONTENTS

CHAPTER ONE
You can have a healthy mind

Many today are suffering what is commonly known as a "nervous breakdown," bogging down in emotional quagmires, utterly failing to get the most out of life, experiencing what can only be called terrifying defeat. It seems vitally important to consider some prophylactic measures that we hope may prevent this tragedy from happening to us. Some physicians believe more than 60 percent of their patients have emotional problems at the core of their physical problems. Others believe this could be as high as 85 percent!

Often, because we do not really understand what a nervous breakdown is, myths tend to grow up around it. It is said that a nervous breakdown is caused by too much work, or that its victim had a mother who ruined his life, or that a nervous breakdown is the logical outcome of the sensitive person's operating in a cruel world, or that a breakdown would never occur if the troubled person would stop thinking about himself. However, according to the best psychology, all these beliefs are, for the most part, untrue.

A nervous breakdown is actually the consequence of an emotional disturbance. Frequently this disturbance is induced by a profound disappointment or by a blow to one's self-esteem. The person who suffers is not crazily out of his mind, but his way of looking at the world has become distorted, and he cannot rightly relate himself to people or responsibility. Regardless of how he was able to cope before, his world is now turned upside down. Consequently, he will become tense and anxious, perhaps feel weak and dizzy, or he may become so depressed that he fears he is losing sanity. He may not be able to sleep, or he may feel drained of all energy. All in all he feels unable to cope with life. When there are disappointments, this person will see tragedy; where there are obstacles, he will see hopeless defeat.

How the one who experiences a nervous breakdown copes with his feelings is another story, and it depends a great deal upon the acuteness of his problem. For example, he may become depressed and experience true amnesia, compulsions, or obsessions. He may quit his job, engage in strange behavior, surrender his responsibilities, or physically collapse. It is important to understand, however, that what has upset him are his inner conflicts and his personal reactions to events, rather than any actual objective circumstance. The values, attitudes, and background of a person can tell us much about the reason for his so-called breakdown.

It is my conviction that the greatest textbook on psychology is the *New Testament* and that it is no meaningless cliché to say that *Christ is the answer.* Dr. Henry C. Link, in his classic book *The Return to Religion,* states that there was nothing sensational or dramatic about his conversion. The change was gradual, and one that he was unaware of for a long time. It was due entirely to the routine experiences encountered in his profession. He continues that as a psychologist he has examined, advised, or assisted in advising over four thousand individuals during the past fifteen years. These people included men and women, the young, the old, the rich, the poor, but with few exceptions they were normal people with normal problems that most of us face at one time or another. Most were dissatisfied with their jobs, their marriages, or their social lives. Many had found themselves in a rut and were considering changing their vocation or getting a divorce. Others had difficulty getting along with others or suffered from an excess of timidity. The education, habits, and discipline of children presented problems, as well as the conflict between religious beliefs and practices, or of obligation to parents or to themselves. Some had undesirable habits they were trying to correct. In short, their difficulties were those of normal people to be dealt with from the standpoint of normal psychology. They were not psychopathic cases to be treated with abnormal or morbid psychology.

Dr. Link further relates that in his dealings with problems of human relationships and behavior, he found himself turning more frequently to the Bible and using biblical expressions, or summing up certain recommendations in terms of accepted Christian doctrines. (Jay E. Adams, author of *Competent to Counsel,* calls this "nouthetic counseling"—based on Scriptural teaching and involvement.) This tendency, Dr. Link explained, sprang from a growing realization that his professional and scientific vocabulary was not always adequate; it was neither clear nor definite enough for the needs of the people he counseled. (This points up the basic weakness of Eric Berne's and Thomas Harris's *Transactional Analysis* and Glasser's *Reality Therapy,* for they are man-centered, not God-centered; their thesis is that the ultimate source for change is *man,* not God.)

Vital Christianity is the answer to the psychopathic mess this world is in, because it is God-centered in that its therapy is found in revelation. Dr. J. A. Hadfield, one of England's foremost psychiatrists, rightly stated that the Christian religion is an extremely valuable and potent influence for producing the harmony, peace of mind, and confidence of soul so needed to bring health and power to those who suffer nervous disorders.

There is a definite reason why the human engine is overheated and why every other bed in the hospitals of the world is filled with a neurotic—to say nothing of the neurotics all around us; for most of us are neurotic to some degree. There are many deep-seated emotional disorders whose origins lie far beneath the level of the conscious mind for which the victim is no more responsible than for some inherited constitutional, bodily disease. But the discovery of vital Christianity as revealed in

12

Jesus Christ could save many from an unhappy existence, ineffectual living, a sense of alienation and rejection, feelings of inadequacy—*and* from the psychiatrist's office. Our matchless Christ, in the majesty of his deity as the Savior of the world, offers us the salvation adequate to all our needs—morally, spiritually, mentally, and emotionally. Christianity is adequacy, and it proposes a life style in which one actually lives life at its very best with tremendous resources, a sense of purpose and a relationship with others that is wholesome and helpful, and which, in many cases, can forestall the need of psychiatry.

One factor in this life style is tranquility of soul, or peace of mind. Undoubtedly the most glorious legacy the Lord Jesus Christ left the world is the promise of John 14:27: "I am leaving you with a gift—peace of mind and heart! And the peace I give isn't fragile like the peace the world gives." Again he declared, "I have told you all this so that you will have peace of heart and mind. Here on earth you will have many trials and sorrows; but cheer up, for I have overcome the world" (John 16:33). Our Lord is speaking here of the peace of *adequate resources.*

It is sad that in this disturbing, upset world, many people have no place within themselves where they can calmly and meditatively retreat and recuperate. We can get ourselves into such a maze of activities that finally we have no idea what to do with our solitariness except to run away from it. Someone has facetiously remarked, "The Japanese commit 'hari-kari'; Americans commit

13

'hurry-scurry'!" Activity without receptivity, the emotional effect of such peaceless living, is utterly disastrous. How desperately we need a quiet oasis in our lives, a place of prayer and communion with God that will charge our spiritual batteries!

The Word of God declares, "He will keep in perfect peace all those whose thoughts turn often to the Lord..." (Isa. 26:3). There is nothing more necessary to the well-being of personality and to a balanced emotional life than this inner security. When the whole world seems to be coming apart at the seams, with time pressing, eternity pulling, and everything about us exploding, this peace can be ours because of the validity of our relationship with Jesus Christ. This is the peace the apostle was speaking of when he wrote to the Philippian Christians, "His peace will keep your thoughts and your hearts quiet and at rest as you trust in Jesus Christ" (Phil. 4:7).

Another factor in this life style is nobility of mind, or good will. Psychiatrists' offices are filled with people who, behind smiling, amiable faces, have for years cherished grudges, nourished hidden anger, and bedeviled themselves with fiendish jealousy. The real cause of such feelings is sometimes concealed even from the one who feels them, and only the deep penetration of the Holy Spirit can uncover and remove them.

A candidate for a nervous breakdown is usually frustrated and is in part angry with himself for feeling so helpless. Repressed ill will transfers itself to any one who crosses the victim's path, and it is conveniently used as an alibi. All responsibility for failure is loaded off on someone else against whom animosity builds up and accumulates. An unhappy, miserable, critical, selfish man hates himself, and he projects that hate to others. But when he surrenders to Christ and recognizes that "there is someone in your hearts who is stronger than any evil teacher in this wicked world" (1 John 4:4), then he can rise above anger, resentment, fear, vengeance, selfishness, and self-pity. But only Christ can give him that power! 1 John 5:4 tells us, "For every child of God can obey him, defeating sin and evil pleasure by trusting Christ to help him." When a man rises above such destructive emotions he is rewarded right here and now by an inward healthiness that makes life beautiful and that cannot be spoiled!

It has been said, "Magnanimity is medicine, and the one person in the world we should really envy is the one who has been delivered completely from the hell of envy"! Far from being an impractical ideal, good will—even toward the ungrateful and hostile—is an indispensable factor in mental and emotional health.

Another factor in the pattern of a healthy emotional life is self-respect. Self-criticism is essential; but we are in a bad state if self-contempt takes charge of us and we view ourselves as utterly worthless. We must *like ourselves*—not in the sense of an exaggerated, blown-up ego, but in an honest evaluation of what we really are. The Apostle Paul said that men should love their wives as they love themselves (Eph. 5:25). Without apology he said, "You should follow my example..." (1 Cor. 11:1).

What he meant was simply that we should have a projected self-image that we can respect.

There is a fantastic temptation to pretend we are invincible, when we know we are not. Many who seem proud, cocky, and arrogant are merely using that as a front to conceal the fact that they are actually sick in soul and despise themselves. Many egotistical people are really not egotistical at all. Their so-called egotism is merely bravado, a front under which they are covering a sense of guilt, inadequacy, humiliation, even self-loathing and hatred.

A narrow, legalistic interpretation of the Scriptures can potentiate this terrible misery. One reason psychology is so often suspicious of and even hostile towards so-called religion is that they see so many cases where it produces silly, irrational remorse over peccadilloes, frightens people with threatened penalties for breaking nonsensical codes, and results in complexes for which there is no sound reason and, I might add, in most instances, no solid, valid, biblical reason. We are not to be controlled by the narrow, often senseless opinions of others. I make one resolution each year: I determine that I will not allow people to make me feel guilty for things about which I should not feel guilty.

The only cure for the perversions of the Christian faith is *true* Christianity with its concept of the believer's glorious position in Christ as seen in the book of Ephesians. If we really know the truth about our position in Christ, we are delivered from the bondage of mere opinion and narrow

16

legalism. When a man believes he is a worthless failure, similar to the leper who believed in the power of Christ but who thought our Lord would not consider him worthy of help, that man can release himself from all responsibility and conclude that there is no use trying because deep down he feels he has no real talents or abilities—or acceptance with God. How the enemy of our souls delights to use this powerful weapon against us! If he can push us into the abyss of despair, our witness is destroyed. If not arrested by time or insight, this kind of feeling can be very destructive to personality and can easily result in severe emotional disturbances. Vital, biblical Christianity as revealed in Christ forever destroys the alibi— "There is no use trying"—because we know that whatever we accomplish it does not depend upon *us* anyway; it depends upon *him*. The Apostle Paul had it right when he said, "... when I am weak, then am I strong" (2 Cor. 12:10). "For I can do everything God asks me to with the help of Christ who gives me the strength and power" (Phil. 4:13). This is a mysticism that cynical, unbelieving psychologists reject as unreal, as mere fantasy. But the trusting believer has discovered beyond all possible doubts the solid truth of the apostle's inspired promise.

Self-respect causes us to discipline ourselves, and discipline causes us to grow and mature into the full stature of the manhood and womanhood God meant us to have, the Christ-likeness we ought to exemplify! Feelings of inadequacy often bring about destructive behavior and contradict

17

our faith. Christianity is sanity! In fact, the whole purpose of redemption is to bring us into a higher, holier relationship than we have ever known, to make our state the complement of our position in Christ. This is the whole work of the Holy Spirit within us, to conform us to the image of the Son (Rom. 8:29). The Word of God says we are "his children ... all God gives to his Son Jesus is now ours too" (Rom. 8:17). We are temples of the Holy Spirit (1 Cor. 3:16). If I have been redeemed and am indwelt by the Holy Spirit and have the assurance that some day I am going to be like Jesus Christ, then, believe me, I must hold my head high so that the world can see him in me! With this kind of a self-image and self-respect there is a good possibility that I may not be found in a psychiatrist's office!

Another factor in the pattern of a truly healthy life style is unselfish devotion to Christ and to others. A self-centered life means an undeveloped, infantile self. There is a principle that Jesus used more than any other, and it is one that *life* uses more than any other: "... anyone who keeps his life for himself shall lose it; and anyone who loses his life for me shall find it again" (Matt. 16:25). This is an eternal law written into the constitution of our beings. Center yourself on your self and you won't like the self you are centered on. Excessive egocentricity is a disease. This is one reason "neurotics" are generally not underprivileged but privileged people with plenty to live *by* and all too often nothing worth living *for*. It is only when we lose ourselves in Christ that we really find ourselves. It is only as we become like Christ that we find the abundant life Christ promised. I have met people whose only goal in life was being Number One. Their life game was "I'm better than you." Deep down they felt they had constantly to prove themselves, and because of this their pedestal positions above others were always joyless. Such men and women are often admired by our culture and may live their lives without any obvious problems. Often their lives may not have much meaning, but still they are envied. One day, however, I am afraid that whatever they accomplished may be classified, as far as their own souls are concerned, as "sticks, and hay, or even straw" (1 Cor. 3:12). Sometimes, at the end of the journey, they realize how empty their existence really was; their lives can be summed up in the hollow phrase—"only leaves" (Mark 11:13).

Underneath the factors in the pattern for a healthy life is one more basic still—the belief that life has direction, meaning, and purpose, that it is not a meaningless jangle, but is going somewhere. Jesus said, "My purpose is to give life in all its fullness" (John 10:10). Do we really believe that faithfulness is all that God requires, that God has a plan for our lives, and that our greatest joy should be simply to be in his will? The Apostle Paul said, "Not that I was ever in need, for I have learned how to get along happily whether I have much or little. I know how to live on almost nothing or with everything. I have learned the secret of contentment in every situation, whether it be a full stomach or hunger, plenty or want; for I can do everything God asks me to with the help of Christ who gives me the strength and power" (Phil. 4:11-13). He advised Timothy, "But godliness with contentment is great gain..." (1 Tim. 6:6, KJV). Discontentment is deadly. If we can honestly say that our "life is in heaven with Christ and God" (Col. 3:3), then we do not need to have futilitarian ideas about life, or even about our present circumstances.

Frequently we are victimized by a compulsive need to be perfect. This feeling operates when we forget the fact that all humans have weaknesses and limitations. Jesus admonished, "Here on earth you will have many trials and sorrows..." (John 16:33). So many times we can only respect ourselves when we are in full command of a situation, when everything is one hundred percent perfect, and therefore we hold ourselves back from what we could do in order to retain the grandiose mental picture we have of ourselves. The perfectionist drives himself cruelly, criticizes himself severely, and forces himself into a breakdown. *Admit* that you make mistakes; don't try to maintain an image that is purely fictional!

In one of my pastorates a well-meaning man came to see me. He knew that I was changing some things, had some new ideas—some of them a bit drastic in his eyes. Standing by my desk he kindly pointed his finger and said with genuine concern, "You're new here, and there's one thing you can't afford to do, and that is to make a mistake."

I answered, "I want to tell you something interesting. I am absolutely confident that in all the years you have had contact with ministers you have never met one that makes as *many* mistakes as I do. I'm just beginning my ministry here, and I'm probably going to make many mistakes. But did you ever stop to think that if I'm right fifty-one percent of the time, things are bound to go quite well?"

I'll never forget how he seemed a little bit awed. Probably by now he knows I was telling the truth! But, you see, in being honest with him, I was immediately released from the bondage in which he was unwittingly attempting to place me.

Demanding tasks and endurances, plus an inner consciousness of inadequacy adds up to a breakdown. When the situation gets bigger than you are, or when you merely *think* the situation is bigger than you are, and you cannot meet it, then the crash comes—a valve breaks and a fuse blows! The strain of modern life makes inner reserves of faith, courage, stability, and endurance critically necessary. Nothing would do more to keep us from needing the help of a psychiatrist than a renewal of intelligent faith in Jesus Christ. There is in Christ a power that will make us adequate to meet life strongly and able to endure its strains and storms. In the great faith chapter in the book of Hebrews we have the marvelous statement about those whose contact with God in explicit trust paid magnificent dividends. The Word of God says, "These people all trusted God and as a result won battles, overthrew kingdoms, ruled their people well, and received what God had promised them; they were kept from harm in a den of lions, and in a fiery furnace. Some, through their faith, escaped death by the sword. Some were made strong again after they had been weak or sick. Others were given great power in battle; they made whole armies turn and run away" (Heb. 11:33, 34). These noble souls had adequate resources for triumphant living.

Dr. Louis Wolberg, medical director of the New York postgraduate center for mental health, offers these suggestions which will help us to a happier, more meaningful life, perhaps see us through the bad times and enhance the good times:

1. Recognize character traits in yourself such as hostility, perfectionism, etc., and try to analyze their effect upon your life.

2. Realize that sometimes a simple change of environment, a new interest in music, a new home, etc., will do wonders for your morale.

3. Start being less passive. Instead of being negative, do something you have been afraid to try or have been putting off. Mobilize your own resources; get excited about your work!

4. Realize that the past is not the present. The self-pitying adult who cries about his unhappy past is a common sight today. People who know a little bit about psychology seem to feel that one's childhood leaves scars from which no one can recover. However, this is only partially true in some cases. More often, by citing their awful past, these people are rationalizing their errors today. As a mature adult you are not responsible for an unhappy childhood, but you are responsible for

dragging that past into the present and reliving your old, unhappy patterns. In other words, you may have been beaten down in childhood, but that does not mean you should remain there. Self-pity is a crippling emotion with practically no virtues, and it is the most powerful destroyer of healthy personality. To harp and harp on one's past is an indulgence you cannot afford. It can only poison your present life.

5. Realize that you can regulate your tensions. The first thing to do is to analyze why you are tense, then you will feel less helpless and can begin to develop a sense of mastery over the frightening situation—a mastery that is the opposite of anxiety. Moreover, ask yourself if your tensions are not self-created. An injustice collector (and some of us are just that!) cannot live without imagined or self-provoked insults.

6. Realize that some frustration and deprivation are essential parts of life. No player hits the ball every time. As one man noted, "You win some, you lose some, and some are rained out."

7. Work at fighting a hopeless attitude. To keep working away is often the key to success. You must believe that things can change and that people can change. And if you believe in God, then you know that they can change. God said, "Ask me and I will tell you some remarkable secrets about what is going to happen here" (Jer. 33:3). We should develop a spirit of expectancy!

8. Exercise willpower. Willpower can help you overcome destructive activities. The Christian, however, has more than willpower; he has the

presence and power of the Holy Spirit guiding and directing him.

9. Stop placing unreasonable demands upon yourself. Learn to analyze and recognize your hostility, perfectionism, or drive to be better than others. Stop worshiping megalomania. Usually you do not have this drive when you want only to do a good job or to test your abilities, but rather because you are meeting some pressure from a parent or competition from peers, or making up for some deeply felt inadequacy. Realize that by setting impossible standards for yourself you will ultimately defeat yourself. Don't center your life on self; center your life on Jesus Christ (Heb. 12:2).

10. Work at building up your self-image. If you feel you are inferior, you will probably unconsciously or consciously increase your dependence on those around you. Instead, focus on your own assets and successes and surrender them to Christ. Most people can succeed at an activity if they are vitally interested in it. People who devalue themselves usually do so because they were taught to, most likely by insecure or unhappy parents, or by siblings who need to belittle those around them in order to enhance their own status. However, you should question this evaluation of yourself, realizing that each of us is unique and blessed with talent. And never forget your position in Christ: you are "accepted in the beloved" (Eph. 1:6, KJV).

11. Ask yourself if you are afraid to be happy. The depressed person sometimes uses his unhappiness to prevent the world from asking him to

assume his fair share of responsibility. As one doctor noted, "Depression is the adult's silent scream." Remember that the depressed person does not give or receive much pleasure. Moreover, he is always attempting to blame others for his misfortunes.

12. Do not place an inordinate amount of hope in the future. In other words, do not live in the future. As Christians, our future is so assured that there is absolutely no reason to worry about it. Matthew 6:34, "Be, therefore, not anxious about tomorrow; for tomorrow will be anxious for the things of itself. Sufficient unto the day is its own evil" (the Greek word for evil here denotes trouble, adversity, or misfortune). Live each day to enjoy *to the maximum* that day!

13. Remember that part of living is being of help to others. As followers of Jesus Christ, it is our responsibility "... not to be served, but to serve ..." (Matt. 20:28). Someone has said, "As long as a person has a wish to be loved without the wish to love, love will elude him." Let the love of Christ saturate your life!

14. Set realistic goals for yourself that will fulfill you. And keep in mind those wonderful words of the apostle, "I can do everything God asks me to with the help of Christ who gives me the strength and power" (Phil. 4:13). Be active! Be alive, excited and enthusiastic! Be, as Peter put it, filled with "the inexpressible joy that comes from heaven itself" (1 Pet. 1:8)! Our real desires in life should be to be in the will of God, to be used by the Spirit of God, and to experience the joy of the

25

Spirit-filled life. These are the real goals that make life glorious and victorious and that can keep us out of the psychiatrist's office!

◆ ◆ ◆

My purpose is to give
life in its fullness.
JOHN 10:10

And he will give them to you
if you give him first place in your life and
live as he wants you to.
MATTHEW 6:33

CHAPTER TWO

How old are you?

The most notable and best known of all the writings of the Apostle Paul is 1 Corinthians 13, the "love chapter" in the book of God's love. Careful consideration reveals that it is a complete treatise on Christian ethics, and more than that, on the philosophy of meaningful living. Actually, 1 Corinthians was written to help immature Christians to spiritual maturity. Certainly nothing is more needed, because emotional and spiritual immaturity are the supreme tragedies of our time. There are altogether too many who are quite mature in age but still victimized by infantile impulses. We find here, as in so many other places, that the Apostle Paul was the forerunner of the best modern psychology.

True science frequently makes discoveries considered recent, only to find that these so-called "discoveries" have been taught in the Bible for centuries. Psychology is a comparatively new science, and much foolishness has been peddled in its name. Much of psychology reminds me of a blind man in a dark room looking for a black cat that isn't there! But it is nevertheless true that a great amount of truth has been established, particularly in the childhood period of life and in discerning the difference between a child's mental processes and those of an adult.

Centuries ago the Apostle Paul said that there are two different sets of mental processes: "When I was a child, I spoke as a child ... I thought as a child; but when I became a man, I put away childish things." Perhaps there is much more profound and practical meaning to this statement than we may have previously discerned. Penetrating teaching is found here, like a lighthouse on a rocky coast, to keep us from disaster as we voyage through life. There are principles and practices of maturity, or, to put it simply, the matter of growing up.

Dr. Earl V. Pierce, now with the Lord for many years, wrote a book that opened up a whole new vista of appreciation for this remarkable chapter in Paul's epistle. Dr. Pierce relates how he discovered in the 11th verse of 1 Corinthians 13 a key to find his own way out of a serious nervous trouble. Three times in his ministry he had a nervous breakdown. Following the first experience he was out of work for six weeks; after the second time he was out of the pastorate for six years. During the first six months of those dark days he was in such melancholia that he did not even smile. After six years he was led by the Lord back into the ministry, but after ten years he was threatened with another breakdown. This time he was sent to a very eminent physician and psychoanalyst under whose direction he studied abnormal psychology. It was then that he discovered a clue to the problem of neurosis: When people are faced with great difficulties, disappointments—something that seems beyond their power or something greatly feared—expression is made through the earlier infantile emotional channels. A nervous breakdown is actually the infant in us crying for some moon which it cannot have, fearing some ghost in the darkness, or resenting some pressure of circumstances. The way out of this difficulty, he suggests, is to learn to recognize this to be a fact. Through this realization, Dr. Pierce was able once again to enjoy an effective ministry. Relatively free from neurosis, he was never again plagued with depressive symptoms.

It is not an exercise of willpower when we are confronted with neurotic symptoms and expressions, but simply a realization that it is the infantile element in us coming to the fore, getting control and dominating us. When we recognize this and move away from infantile reactions to more mature behavior, we find that we are "cured."

The law of the infant is the law of the animal, the law of impulse: I want what I want when I want it, and if I don't get it I'll raise a ruckus. During this early period a little child only thinks of himself. He is self-centered, fantastically egocentric and therefore self-disruptive. He is oblivious, unappreciative, and unable to perceive of any interest besides or outside of himself. By nature, except when restrained or threatened, he is impatient, often cruel, boastful, immodest, selfish, will-

29

ful, untruthful, disobedient, self-pitying; but these things are to be expected. He will pout, scream, make a scene, do anything he feels like doing upon any given occasion. All the elements of love are in reverse.

Paul gives us the assurance that when he was an infant he had precisely these characteristics. And when we were infants so did we. Our basic, physical drives and instincts controlled us; our judgments and desires were all on a physical basis. A child that is consistently gracious and good tempered is a very welcome exception to what we have a right to expect.

Because an infant follows sense reaction, his guides are simply pleasure and pain, satisfaction and dissatisfaction. His likes and dislikes, rather than reason or authority, govern his behavior. In his manifestation he is an animal—sweet, lovable, endearing—but interested only in himself, and governed by basic instincts. He seeks what he wants and makes trouble when he does not get it. The language he understands is the language of the flesh. Therefore, spanking or other slightly painful experiences are God-given processes to correct infantile impulses. In this situation, a small measure of pain is very useful as a guide, because it is the one means of control a child really understands.

As a child grows, authority should increasingly be the governing control. Law must gradually be injected into a child's consciousness through the rules of the home, the church, the school, and the Bible. A child must realize that there are certain people who love him and who take care of him and thus have the right to tell him what to do and what not to do. Childhood is the period for developing discipline.

Dr. Link, in his book *The Return to Religion,* emphasizes that the prime necessity for a well-developed emotional life and a well-developed character is the careful and consistent application of sensible, thoughtful, loving discipline. The late J. Edgar Hoover tells us that this is the most needful factor in juvenile life today. It is explicit that the foundation in developing respect for authority must be established in infancy. Psychologists tell us that if a child does not learn to yield his will to that of another before he learns to talk, he will never do so apart from compulsion. Liberal radicals, rabid anarchists, fanatical crusaders, yippies, hippies and purveyors of violence, who violate laws as they please, are really full grown infants who have been nurtured in a permissive atmosphere and have had their own way from the beginning. A judge once said that preparation for the electric chair often begins in the high chair.

Childhood is too early to expect reason to be a complete guide, and because it is not safe to let mere impulse be the guide, the will of the parent and teacher should be dominant, kindly, loving, and firm. Many of our young people grow up with only one valid source of guidance—a TV set. *Parade* magazine recently observed that in the first eighteen years the average child in the United States spends 22,000 hours watching television. Since the end of World War II, American children

31

have logged more time watching video than they have in reading, writing, playing outdoors or talking to their parents.

Fighting Sam Hayakawa, the semanticist and highly publicized "pepper-pot" president of San Francisco State College, feels that television helped set the stage for youth's contemporary rebellion and behavior pattern. He makes the point that the viewer need only sit silent and passive while the little box spews out a fountain of entertainment, commercials, and information. You never interact with a television set; you never relate to it; you simply turn it on. He feels that young people who have spent so much time watching TV cannot effectively relate to people around them, thus widening the generation gap. Eventually they become incapable of relating reasonably to anyone but themselves, and many of them have divided personalities such that they cannot relate even to themselves. They have a loss of identity.

Further, he maintains that television teaches a simplistic technique of problem solving. If you want to marry a beautiful girl, use the right deodorant. If you want to be very, very masculine, use a certain brand of shaving lotion, and so on. With rebellion and knowledge, young people finally reject these "hucksters'" teachings, but they are imbued with the infantile processes of thinking and they expect problems to have a one-step, one-word, thirty-minute solution.

Furthermore, with the usual fantastic lack of syntax in television, the time element in achievement is ignored. In Scene I a young man wants to be a doctor; in Scene II he *is* a doctor. Drugs are the natural refuge of a child nurtured and matured on television. The kinship is obvious. Both depend upon turning on and passively waiting for something beautiful and exciting to happen. Hayakawa says that the "super-babysitter" has backfired. God never meant a television set to determine the destiny of our young people. It may be the real culprit that has warped our generation.

Again, television honors and solves problems by violence. Undoubtedly, this has contributed to the fact that there are 6,500 murders in the United States every year. In contrast, where there is tight government control and supervision of television programming, there are far fewer murders every year: 30 in England, 99 in Canada, 68 in Germany, and 37 in Japan. In 1967 two million guns were sold in the United States. In 1968 there were 74,241 pistols sold in California. Every day two children under five years of age are killed by their parents. Every hour five are seriously injured. We are a fantastically violent nation, and perhaps television is responsible! *TV Guide,* in an article entitled "The Triggered, the Obsessed and the Schemers" (February 2, 1974), reported a dozen criminal and antisocial acts, all inspired by TV. The most gruesome concerned Evelyn Wagler, who was forced to throw gasoline over herself, then was set afire by Boston ghetto teenagers. Police officials recalled immediately that her death was parallel to that of a scene in a movie on TV two nights before, called *Fuzz.* In the film, teenage boys were shown setting derelicts afire just for

33

fun. A few days after the Boston murder, a similar event took place in Miami when three boys, two aged thirteen and one twelve, set fire to a derelict.

Psychologically, one who has emerged thoroughly from the infantile period into a healthy, normal childhood, respecting authority, is well girded for the future and is not likely to become one of the neurotics who has a breakdown and "enjoys poor health." But if he is lacking discipline and is nurtured in permissiveness there is trouble ahead. According to the latest statistics, one out of every six children entering school has a nervous breakdown, because for the first time in his life he cannot run things. This is a pitiable tragedy for a child, and one that wise parents could and should prevent. The characteristics of full maturity come when one embraces the matchless Christ in an intimate, life-transforming experience as the Lord of life, and then becomes a "slave of Jesus Christ." In other words, he surrenders to an ultimate authority as his life figure and guide.

When beyond the infantile period there occurs any blocking of life—of its ambitions or purposes, the loss of property, of a loved one, of health, when one finds himself unable to cope with a situation—the tendency is for the emotions to back up and express themselves through the earlier, large outlets made in the infant period. This may be, for example, the temporary giving way to childish reactions, which may easily develop into what is called the neurotic or the infantile impulse. The mature, spiritually adequate person is the one who accepts reality, who, as one physician ex-

34

pressed it, makes the best of it—"smiling, even if you are going to be hung."

Love bears all things; it endures, stands up under circumstances, and does not give way. It patiently waits for the better day. Realizing that better days are ahead, the Christian should hold steady, not with the cold granite of stoicism, but with the strong courage of a vital, valid faith. And we must come to grips with the truth that neurotic conditions and nervous breakdowns, all the way from the blues to suicide, are an infantile attempt to escape reality instead of adjusting oneself reasonably to reality. (This is the principal thesis of "Reality Therapy," a major breakthrough in psychiatry born of the dissatisfaction with the ineffectiveness and unreality of the types of psychiatry and psychology which, in effect, dismiss morality from the focus of treatment. The new psychiatry and psychology hold people responsible for their behavior.)

We are launched at birth from a protected and dependent existence to an exposed life that must become more and more independent. From the moment we are dashed into the ocean of life, we raise a cry of protest, and we continue to do so until we finally learn to swim. The person who does not become neurotic is the one who can bless each wave that hits him with, "I got through that one, and if I did, I can make the next one," and comes out on the other side with a smile. The neurotic, on the other hand, is the one who keeps up the first infant howl with each new obstacle he faces in life. By the time a person has matured physically, he should also have matured psychologically, and most important of all—spiritually. Animal, primitive, infantile impulses should be under the control of our God-given reason and, above that, the Holy Spirit—the Spirit of Wisdom who has been given to guide and direct us. Thus we would do what is helpful, right, and mature.

In summation, there is a marked, radical difference between the infantile and mature states in a moral, social, and spiritual way, as well as physical. The infantile state has its place. We expect a baby to be no different from what he is. We put up with him, though he often requires painful adjustment on our part. We expect him to be pre-eminently an animal, albeit a very precious one. We do not look for judgment, reason, self-control, or self-sacrifice. We expect him to be thoroughly self-centered and to have selfishness as his prime motive except as he is trained away from this. For parents to indulge the infantile impulse is to spoil the child, and this spoiling is simply the result of our neglecting to take the trouble to overcome these selfish, animalistic (the New Testament word would be "fleshly") tendencies. This is undoubtedly the battle the Apostle Paul describes when he speaks of the flesh warring with the spirit, and he reminds us that it is a never-ending battle.

This battle, however, is actually the whole work of God with man: to lift him out of the infantile and the "fleshly" into the heavenly plane of values and relationships we find through our commitment to Jesus Christ. Or, to use a dispensational expression, to make our state nearer our position in Christ. The goal of the Holy Spirit, the revelation of God's will through the prophets and apostles and through his Son, the coming of our Lord, forgiveness of sin, justification, regeneration, sanctification, the dedication and commissioning of parents to bring up their children in the nurture and admonition of the Lord—all the agencies of the Christian revelation—have as their purpose the subduing of the animal, infantile, selfish, carnal part of our nature. They are guides to bring us to spiritual maturity, helping us to become more like Jesus Christ and to discover our particular place of serving in the Spirit. These are the goals of salvation. Man is living like an animal, but he was created for something higher. The animal nature was given to man only to give him force—never to rule him.

The classic passage of 1 Corinthians 13 sets forth this goal of spiritual maturity. In it is a detailed presentation of the conduct God is seeking to bring about in all of us. It is not the number of years that counts, but how grown up we are emotionally and spiritually. In this respect it is interesting that our Lord is called the "Ancient of Days" (Dan. 7:9). This is a beautiful declaration of his perfection. He is perfect in love, which means he is completely mature. He is everything in maturity that we desire to be. We can determine our emotional and spiritual age by the very same principles.

There are seventeen characteristics the Apostle Paul gives us in the 13th chapter of 1 Corinthians concerning love—some positive, some negative—but, as Dr. Pierce suggests, we can combine them under eight separate headings. From these we can discover how old we are emotionally and spiritually, how far we are removed from being victims of infantile impulses. We may discover that we are older in years but infantile in character.

1. *Patience.* The apostle says that love suffers long, is not easily provoked, bears all things and endures all things. James 1:4 (KJV) says that perfect patience makes a perfect person: "... let patience have her perfect work, that ye may be perfect and entire, lacking nothing." The word "perfect" does not mean ethical holiness, but maturity, the highest development of which we are capable. Our Lord, in the Sermon on the Mount, urges us to be loving in the treatment of our enemies. He said, in Matthew 5:48, "But you are to be perfect, even as your Father in heaven is perfect." "Perfect" is the Greek word *teleios.* It denotes an end accomplished, the completion of a practice. This is equivalent to telling us that we are to be full grown, to be mature, to be Godlike.

With Paul, patience is such a first and cardinal grace that he presents four characteristics of love that can be called by that beautiful term. Patience is the very flower of a fine personality, of the 24-karat gold character. None of these could we ever find in an infant. An infant does not suffer long, but screams with the first pain. The moment there is pain there is protest. Unless the pain is removed the anger escalates. A child has a very limited tension capacity. Tension capacity is the time element

38

between desire and fulfillment. With a child there is absolutely no elasticity; desire and fulfillment are one.

How about your tension capacity? How long can you wait? How much elasticity do you have? This will tell us how old we are. Patience marks us as mature.

Consider the patience of Adoniram Judson (1788-1850), missionary to Burma. Feeling the call of God to preach and teach the gospel to the Burmese, it was necessary, first of all, for him to learn the difficult Burmese language. At that time the language had no written grammar. For three years he worked on the grammar. It was six months after this that he preached in Rangoon, his first sermon in Burmese. It was six years later that he baptized his first convert. He suffered incredible hardships, but never gave up. In fact, he took his first furlough after *thirty years* of service! For all these years he saw very little fruit for all of his labor. Nevertheless, he characterized in his life the magnificent virtue of patience. Following his death, the seed he had so faithfully planted brought forth a harvest of souls.

Notice the words Paul uses: *suffer, bear, endure.* How vividly and dramatically these words are seen in the life and ministry of the Lord Jesus Christ! How infinitely removed he was from the selfish impulses of infantilism, or, to use the apostle's words, "the flesh." How governed he was by reason, by the Holy Spirit. Think of the noble characters you have known, and you will discover they were like our Lord in this respect.

39

One element of patience deserves to be considered by itself. The apostle says that love is not
provoked. The most accurate meaning here is,
"Love does not get provoked." In other words,
love does not feel vengeful. It does not feel like
slapping back, which is seen in the animal when it
bites, or in the child when he slaps and scratches.
It is seen in the grown-up "infant" when he shoots
forth bitter words or engages in venomous attack.
What is more tragic in a home than to see a helpless baby or an irresponsible child enslaved by a
petulant, irascible, infant adult? This infantile lack
of patience, a lack of Christ-like maturity, is seen
in us when our pride is hurt or when we are
crossed in some way, and we *react* instead of
thoughtfully act. When we do this we are babies
ourselves, infants having a tantrum. And if you
have a heart condition, that tantrum could cost
you your life.

How old are you by the pattern of patience?

2. *Kindness.* This is a word seldom heard any
more. It is almost lost to our culture. Real love is
kind. The apostle tells us in Ephesians 4:32, "... be
kind to each other...." A child is often cruel, if by
cruelty he can achieve his ends. He will bite,
scratch, shove, push—whatever seems necessary
to get what he wants. The Golden Rule is the rule
of emotional and spiritual maturity. That is why so
few follow it. This is an unkind world. Meanness
and cruelty are infantile facets in us. A study of
tyrannical dictators dramatically reveals that they
are emotionally immature; they are simply
grown-up infants. When we have grown into the

40

likeness of Christ, into the stature of manhood and womanhood in him, maturity takes the place of infancy, and the Spirit takes the place of the flesh. Love supplants selfishness, and kindness comes in the place of cruelty. The apostle tells us that when the fruit of the Spirit is in evidence, there is actually no necessity of law.

How beautiful is the fruit of the Spirit, outlined in Galatians 5:22, 23 (KJV): "... the fruit of the Spirit is love, joy, peace, long-suffering [patience], gentleness, goodness, faith, meekness, self-control; against such there is no law." These are the characteristics of the Spirit-filled, Spirit-guided, Spirit-controlled life. These are the marks of maturity, and the lack is the mark of the infant.

How old are you by the standard of kindness?

When we allow something less than the matchless Christ to take the central place in our loyalty and affection, we cannot avoid the inevitable influences which offset the fruits of the Spirit. These subversive influences, because they are infantile, produce a rigid, inflexible, brittle character that can easily "break down."

The secret of Christian growth is summed up in four verses by the apostle: Romans 8:1-4 (KJV): "There is, therefore, now no condemnation to them who are in Christ Jesus, who walk not after the flesh, but after the Spirit [remember, flesh is infantile; spirit is mature]. For the law of the Spirit of life in Christ Jesus hath made me free from the law of sin and death. For what the law could not do, in that it was weak through the flesh, God sending his own Son, in the likeness of sinful flesh

41

and for sin, condemned sin in the flesh [condemned the infantile], that the righteousness of the law might be fulfilled in us, who walk not after the flesh, but after the Spirit." When we experience the joy of spiritual maturity in Christ, we are no longer victimized by emotional immaturity.

3. *Generosity,* or magnanimity. Paul writes that love envies not. Envy has been defined as selfish ill will toward another because the other possesses that which we want or has achieved something we have always desired to achieve and have not done so. It is ill will toward a person because he has either been favored more than we, or else we are convinced that he is superior to us.

Envy is a marked characteristic of infancy and childhood. A little child wants whatever pleases him, and if you happen to possess what he wants he will hate you if you don't give it up. This is a common animal characteristic. The dog is jealous if you pet the cat. If a little child is allowed to continue in his selfishness, he will resent the intrusion of a new baby. One such youngster complained petulantly to his mother, because the baby was taking up her time, "I wish it had a mama of its own!"

There is no more insidious sin that threatens the lives of adults than the sin of envy. This sin is more penetrating and prevalent than most of us like to admit. To recognize envy for its own age—the impulse of an infant—is to become ashamed of it and to set it aside. It was Henry Drummond who said that the only one we should really envy is the one who envies not. Whenever a person reacts with irritation at someone superior, envy has begun its malignant work. Envy always stems from a sense of inferiority. Envy says, "You are superior to me." Someone has suggested that the difference between envy and jealousy is that *envy* begins with empty hands, mourning its lack, but joying when others lose their superiority. *Jealousy* begins with full hands, fearful of losing what it has to someone else. Envy stands at the bottom of the pile, breathing ill will at the king of the castle; jealousy stands at the top of the heap, fearful that someone is going to take its place. Jealousy is our fear over or because of superiority; envy is our uneasiness under it.

The Apostle Paul says that love rejoices with those who rejoice. If it cannot have certain things itself, it is glad to see others enjoy them. Happy people are those free from the spirit of envy. For example, let's assume you have always wanted a Cadillac but could never afford one, and then your neighbor gets one. If you can honestly be glad and happy for him, you have conquered envy.

How old are we by the gauge of generosity? How much can we enjoy blessings that come to others but that don't come to us? We are completely delivered from envy when we can vicariously identify with someone else's achievement and someone else's acquisition, and so identify with him that our joy is equal to his. This is maturity.

4. *Modesty* is another characteristic of maturity. Paul mentions three things that can be grouped together under modesty: Love vaunteth not itself,

is not puffed up, and does not behave itself unseemly. Immodesty unnecessarily seeks to draw attention to itself. In this respect, how obvious is the contrast between the infantile and the mature. A little child has no modesty; he vaunts himself, he struts. He wants to be the center of attention and will perform all kinds of stunts to get that attention. He will cry, make a noise, or break in on a conversation. Dr. William Sadler says that there is in all young children a tendency to exhibit themselves. In every walk of life there are those who strut, who seek to draw attention to themselves, who are inflated with an exaggerated egotism and who behave so that others are embarrassed. As was suggested by the late C. S. Lewis, however, the more you see of egotism in others the more you have of it yourself, because it is competitive.

Self-pity is one of the unseemly things. There are those who delight in posing as martyrs. They are always telling how badly they've been abused, mistreated, and misunderstood. No one knows what they've had to bear and certainly no one has ever borne what they have. They can carefully document point for point how they have been wronged, and carefully delineate all the sins that have been committed against them, yet frequently never see their own.

How unseemly pouting is! Pouting in men and women is not a bit more beautiful than in the child who goes off by himself and sullenly declines to cooperate. Love does not engage in this kind of reaction; it puts it away as childish.

The indulgence of any wrong mood is needless

and a wicked way of giving in to the infantile. Someone has said that Jesus never felt "blue" or depressed because blueness is ingrowing, offended vanity. It is pouting; so don't pout! Realize that this is not mature but infantile. It is the baby in us craving attention, and we must at once shed it as unbecoming and immodest. We need to take a look at ourselves and, by the measure of modesty, discover how old we are.

5. *Unselfishness.* The apostle says that love "seeketh not its own." In other words, love gets what it needs along with others. It looks to the interest of the group and with the group it prospers or does not prosper. Many of us have only to look to our mothers to know how unselfish love can be. But look beyond to the Lord Jesus Christ, the great exemplar of it. Selfishness is infantile. Service is selflessness and is mature. Selfishness is, without a doubt, the most destructive attitude there is—not only to our personality but to our relationship to others as well.

One form of infantile selfishness, which the apostle always describes by the word "flesh," is common stubbornness. Some are never willing to cooperate. If things are not done their way, they will not have any part. Some are so pronounced in this that if you wish to accomplish a certain thing, you may find it wise to propose the very opposite. (This, of course, is playing games. It is compensatory action—appealing to the child in us, not to the adult.)

By the scale of selfishness and unselfishness, how old are you?

6. *Pure minds.* Paul says that love takes no account of evil; it rejoices not in unrighteousness, but in the truth. Love is not suspicious. It does not keep an account book in which it records all the debt due it. Selfish people, who have their minds upon themselves, are sensitive and suspicious. They are always looking for slights and evil things done toward them. They always feel something is going on that isn't right. They distrust leadership and motivation. Sensitive and suspicious people are selfish and therefore infantile.

Love does not rejoice in moral unrighteousness in others. Often we profess horror at evil and yet love to listen to the evil tale so we can pass it on. Gossip and scandalmongers are the supreme egotists. They are full of conceit; they are self-centered. They are stunted natures, bearing in their adulthood all the characteristics of a blighted babyhood. The psychological reaction is this: By professing horror over evil, while still loving to hear about it, and by telling unnecessarily of the evil that someone else has done, they are seeming to say, "See what a righteous person I am, for I am horrified about this evil." This person is telling the tale with a selfish purpose. Here is the tattle-tale child grown up. The mature person buries evil things he may happen to hear and keeps far away from things that are a real horror to him.

Love reckons on what is valuable and necessary for the good of others, and does this on the basis of wisdom. It never tells of unrighteousness unless it is required for the welfare of the group or for society. If we love gossip, we are not very mature.

46

Our newspapers are built on the principle that the majority of its readers are children who in self-righteous pride will smack their lips over the evil that other people are doing. That evil is always considered the best news is a certain indictment of the race as being immature. Often an accusation is printed with blazing headlines, but when the accusation has proven false and the one accused is exonerated, the facts are found in an abbreviated article in small print in the back pages of the paper.

Love rejoices in the truth, for love and truth are one. This basically means that love rejoices in the gospel because this is the way New Testament writers often referred to the gospel—as the "Truth." The verb "rejoices" proves this by its form; literally, "love rejoices together with the truth." Selfishness, with its shortsightedness, is what rejects the gospel, but when we let the Holy Spirit develop in us the love of God, then we receive the gospel. The Apostle Paul says the flesh, the infantile, is enmity against God (Rom. 8:7), and so it is enmity against all that God does. It does not have or like the conviction of sin and the surrender of the flesh that the gospel demands. Becoming a Christian is thus seen to be "growing up," coming to the stature of manhood and womanhood in Christ Jesus. It begins, as it did with Paul, in putting away self-righteousness as a childish thing and accepting justification in Christ, which brings us into fellowship with God. It is the glorious experience of God's grace, of knowing you are "accepted in the beloved" (Eph. 1:6, KJV).

Love rejoices in all truth against untruth. Love tells the truth and loves it in others. A lie is natural to a child if it seems to protect him, and so he resorts to it. It is done through the instinct of self-preservation, which is the first law of the animal life, but it is not the first law of the spiritual life. Truth is the first law of the spiritual life, and we have to be brought up to this. In this respect, there are some who never grow up, who never learn to tell the truth when it suits them to tell a lie or a half-truth, which amounts to a whole lie.

Truth requires courage—moral courage, courage to face what people think. Women, I believe, are more given to lying than men; men are more given to pride, which is actually an overdose of exaggerated ego. This, in itself, often makes them tell the truth. Concern for what other people think, however, often causes men to lie. But whenever the temptation to lie arises, remember that the lie is similar to the cowardly, sneaking instinct of a child's effort to protect himself from undesirable consequences. Tell the truth and prove the Holy Spirit is in control of your life and you have grown up (1 Cor. 6:19).

By the test of truth how old are you?

7. *Optimism.* "Love ... believeth all things, hopeth all things..." Selfishness makes people suspicious, while unselfishness opens up the mind of truth. Love is indeed so believing that it needs the wisdom of the Word of God, of the Holy Spirit, to guide it lest it become credulous. The simple, the open-minded, may learn by experience, but the skeptic becomes hard and impervious to the truth.

48

Because love believes, love hopes. Love has a future; love looks a long way ahead; love sees eternity. The infant on the other hand, sees only the present and lives only in the present. It does not relate to the past or the future. Beliefs play no part in its life. Existentialism is in many ways a form of infantilism because its basic philosophy is the seizing and living for nothing beyond the present moment.

There are those who have no interest in what God has prepared for those who love him. They say, "This world is good enough for me." They are therefore "without God," as the apostle describes the Ephesians before their conversion, being "without hope" (Eph. 2:12). They look at the things that are seen and never at the things that are unseen, reversing Paul's program for gaining blessings from life's afflictions. But the mature Christian looks beyond this world into the next and there is a glorious continuity and eternalness to his existence. He really believes Romans 8:28, "... that all that happens to us is working for our good if we love God and are fitting into his plans." He has a hope "connecting us with God himself behind the sacred curtains of heaven, where Christ has gone ahead to plead for us" (Heb. 6:19, 20), holding him, sustaining him and giving him a tremendous security for all of life. He believes Christ, and this gives him the peace of adequate resources. He lives from the present, but he lives in the assurance of the future and is therefore already partaking of its vastness. This hope blazes forth with what the apostle calls the "blessed hope," the coming of our Lord Jesus Christ. We believe that our Lord will yet, by his own presence and power, do what man is unable to do—overcome evil in this world. We are the true optimists, in a sense—the only optimists, because we endure not only as seeing him who is invisible, but we endure because of the certainty of the epiphany, the bright shining forth of the great King of kings and Lord of lords who is yet to come. Thus, by our optimism, our well-grounded hope in the future, because God is with us and Christ is coming, we can judge our maturity.

8. *Permanence.* "Love never faileth...." The last characteristic of love Paul mentions is permanence. Love is lasting; it never plays out. 1 John 2:17 (KJV) tells us, "... he that doeth the will of God abideth forever." He that doeth the will of self passes away with the infantile life of the present. I like Phillips' translation of 1 John 2:15-17: "Never give your hearts to this world or to any of the things in it. A man cannot love the Father and love the world at the same time. For the whole world system, based as it is on men's primitive desires, their greedy ambitions and the glamour of all that they think splendid, is not derived from the Father at all, but from the world itself. The world and all its passionate desires will one day disappear. But the man who is following God's will is part of the permanent and cannot die."

How fickle is childhood; how quickly it forgets; how short its loves. It rests in its own pleasure, and if it can find pleasure in another, it readily transfers its allegiance. The so-called love of a child can seldom be called more than attachment. He likes, rather than loves. In this respect, some never grow up. They never come to the time when they are devoted to the welfare of those they are supposed to love. When the attachment involves sacrifice, it becomes weakened and breaks.

I wonder how permanent our love really is, or how many times our love is similar to a child's— merely temporary attachment. How well does our love stand the test of time? Permanence is the final test of *all* values. The apostle tells us, "... whether there be prophecies, they shall be done away; whether there be tongues, they shall cease; whether there be knowledge, it shall vanish away. For we know in part, and we prophesy in part. But when that which is perfect is come, then that which is in part shall be done away" (1 Cor. 13:8-10, KJV). The content of knowledge and prophecy that was known in the early Church and recorded in the Word of God will be rendered inoperative when our Lord calls his Church to be with himself. So there is a time when prophecy will be no more, a time when the content of knowledge, as recorded in the Word, will no longer be necessary. But if you love the matchless Christ, you are just at the foot of a great highway that reaches out into the vastness of eternity. There is but one permanent, unshakable, eternal fact in this world and in us, and that is the love of Christ for us and that love shed abroad in our hearts by the Holy Spirit. If you do not love Jesus Christ in that kind of commitment, if you are not devoted to him in a sense of permanent abandonment to

Christ, if you like only *some* of the things about him, put away these childish things and rise up into the maturity of devotion and deathless conviction and commitment to him.

Because our Lord is love and is infinitely mature, we can see the full picture of what Paul is painting by reading it thus: Jesus Christ suffered long and was kind; Jesus Christ envied not; Jesus Christ vaunted not himself, was not puffed up, did not behave himself unseemly, sought not his own, was not provoked, did not take account of evil, rejoiced not in unrighteousness, but rejoiced with the truth. He bore all things, believed all things, hoped all things, endured all things. Jesus never failed, and never will fail.

Reading 1 Corinthians 13 every day for six months transformed the life of Henry Drummond, and it will do the same for anyone. Let us be penetrated and saturated with the love of Christ. When we are, then we will be mature. How wonderful are the words of the Apostle Paul: When he became a man in Christ, he "put away the childish things." So he wrote for us this lyric of love to lead us on, as found in Ephesians 4:11-16 *(Phillips):* "His 'gifts unto men' were varied. Some he made his messengers, some prophets, some preachers of the Gospel; to some he gave the power to guide and teach his people. His gifts were made that Christians might be properly equipped for their service, that the whole body might be built up until the time comes when, in the unity of common faith and common knowledge of the Son of God, we arrive at real maturity—that measure of development which is meant by the 'fullness of Christ.' We are not meant to remain as children, at the mercy of every chance wind of teaching and the jockeying of men who are expert in the crafty presentation of lies. But we are meant to hold firmly to the truth in love, and grow up in every way into Christ, the head. For it is from the head that the whole body, as a harmonious structure knit together by the joints with which it is provided, grows by the proper functioning of individual parts to its full maturity in love."

◆ ◆ ◆

When I was a child
I spoke and thought and reasoned as a child does.
But when I became a man my thoughts grew far beyond
those of my childhood, and now I have put away
my childish things.
1 CORINTHIANS 13:11

CHAPTER THREE

Your inferiority complex—or— meet your Mr. Hyde!

Vital Christianity is not theoretical; it is practical. It is astounding how defeated persons can be changed into triumphant individuals when they really utilize their faith as a workable instrument. I have never seen a situation that could not be marvelously altered by a commitment to the living Christ.

The mature Christian should not see himself as through his own eyes, but as what he is and *can be* through Jesus Christ. There were three persons in Matthew, the publican: the publican whom his associates saw, the Matthew whom Matthew saw, and the Matthew whom Jesus saw. Each of these thought he saw the true Matthew, but of course, the *true* Matthew was the one our Lord saw, and he turned out to be the Matthew of infinite possibilities. Similarly, there are three persons in you: the one your associates see, the outer self; the one you see, the introspective, present self; and the one whom our Lord sees, the future you, the self of infinite possibilities.

Everything in your life depends on which "you"

you center upon. If you are centering on the self your associates see, then you will be in bondage to what others think about you. You will look around before you act to see what effect your action will have on others. In this case, you won't act; you will react. You will become an echo, not a voice; a thing, not a valid person. If you center upon the self you know, then you will be discouraged, for who has not had some skeletons in his closet—things in his life that make his cheeks burn with shame and humiliation. If you are centered on this "self" of self-analysis, you will be caught in the bondage of inhibitions by what you have been and are. But there is that third you, the one our Lord sees. And what a "you" that is! It is the you that surrenders to God, the you that is under the control of the Holy Spirit, the you that is cooperating with him, using his resources and operating in his power. This is the *real* you! Center on Christ's "you" and you will become just that!

Our Lord looks not upon what a man has *been;* he is concerned about what a man is *becoming.* That being true, there is no reason to live under the blight of an inferiority complex, and yet most people do. There is the "you" that you can center your life upon so that you can overcome every obstacle. This is the thesis of Dr. Maxwell Maltz's book *Psycho-Cybernetics.* There is a tendency in human nature to become like the self you imagine yourself to be. The Bible puts it this way: "As [a man] thinketh in his heart, so is he" (Prov. 23:7, KJV). Believe you are defeated—believe it long enough—and it is likely to become a fact, because

55

the image you have of yourself is a defeated image.

People who achieve happiness and success are those who, upon finding themselves sinking into a depressed mood, shake it off by refusing to accept the idea of defeat, because the self image they maintain is one of victory. They refuse to entertain the possibility that situations, circumstances, or their enemies have them down. They know it is more the thought of defeat, the image of defeat, that causes defeat. So they practice thinking positive thoughts and so project a positive image. Thoughts of faith in Christ surge through their minds. The Apostle Paul wrote to the Philippians, "Let this mind be in you, which was also in Christ Jesus..." (Phil. 2:5, KJV). They train their minds to think victoriously, and as a result they become victorious Christians.

Basically, an inferiority complex is a habitual feeling of inferiority to others. It arises from wrong thinking acquired either in childhood or as a result of later experiences. An inferiority complex may be defined as a system of emotionally toned ideas ranged around one central idea— disbelief in oneself. To rob a person of legitimate belief in himself is to do him a grievous wrong. In many cases a suicide would never have taken place if that person's belief in himself had not received a death blow. A man without God finds it hard to believe in himself because he has no ultimate goal. Life for him is a trip to nowhere. Unrelated to anything, he dangles in space until the countdown hits zero, the fuse burns out, and it becomes "boxing day."

An inferiority complex usually begins in childhood. The symptoms can be quickly recognized by the way we tend to compensate; that is, by the method our subconscious mind uses to make up for feelings of inadequacy. If we look at certain types of compensatory behavior we gain a comprehensive idea of how disbelief in oneself, or a poorly projected image of oneself, influences one's behavior.

The following are some of the causes of inferiority complexes that originate in childhood.

1. *Organic disability.* This is a very common cause. When a child is chronically ill, there is a tendency of parents to spoil him because he may be semi-invalid. Because there is no normal outlet for the child, often there results overcompensation in the child, so as to cover his self-conscious sensitiveness with conceit, assertiveness, failure to cooperate, selfishness, etc.

2. *Relation of children in a family to one another.* An inferiority complex is often brought on when one of the children is belittled or minimized, or when the natural inability of the youngest or smallest child is magnified.

3. *Parents have the wrong attitude toward a child and the child feels rejected.* This is often a disastrous tragedy, because the person can be conditioned to experience rejection.

4. *Domination of an overbearing personality.* We should constantly remind ourselves that every little personality whose life touches our own is of infinite worth to God and of greater delicacy and sensitiveness than we realize. If we take the re-

sponsibility of leading, training and guiding, let us have respect for these young personalities and treat them with dignity, courtesy, kindness, and yet with firmness (which is real leadership) and, of course, that humor to which they so readily respond. Let us be ourselves what we wish them to be, because ultimately our children reflect what we are. We cannot too often remind ourselves of those solemn words spoken by our Lord about caring for little children: "But if any of you causes one of these little ones who trusts in me to lose his faith, it would be better for you to have a rock tied to your neck and be thrown into the sea" (Matt. 18:6). "Beware that you don't look down upon a single one of these little children..." (Matt. 10:13), for whatever we think about them, they are regarded as the greatest asset to the kingdom in the eyes of God. Never for a second does God cease to be concerned about them.

Notice some of the characteristics of compensations for an inferiority complex:

1. *Overassertiveness.* The one who overasserts himself struts instead of walks. He is pompous. When he talks it is likely to be in a loud voice, no matter where he is. When he discusses any subject, he gives the impression he knows all there is to know about it. You say, "How conceited he is." Not necessarily. It may be more accurate to say, "How sick he is." He needs his assertiveness because he has a profound feeling of emptiness and inadequacy. His overbearing attitude is the way his mind unconsciously seeks to make up for his terrible feelings of inferiority. Eric Berne would

call it the "I'm not OK—you're OK" feeling. In other words, it is an unconscious effort to "save face." It is his subconscious mind ever attempting to assert itself. Actually, it is "game playing." One who is not sure of himself may talk loudly, boast and swagger to impress others. Thus he attempts to bolster himself with an outward show because of inner unrelieved weakness.

Jesus saw men striving to increase their position or standing among men, so he said, "Which of you by being anxious can add one cubit unto his stature?" (Matt. 6:27, KJV). We try to add cubits to our stature by developing certain external dimensions to compensate for inner inferiority. The psychologist says, "There are a million chances to one that those who claim to be superior are unpopular among those who know them best. And thus they defeat their own purpose." He that saveth his life by concentrating hard on it, by dressing it up to appear bigger than it is, is bound to defeat his own purpose. In the words of Jesus, he "will lose it" (Mark 8:35). Superior attitudes and delusions of grandeur are the reverse side of an inferiority complex, so shun superficial superiority as you would shun the devil, for they are much the same.

Another type of false compensation or overassertiveness is exemplified in the one who always comes late to every gathering in order for everyone to notice him when he arrives, and who leaves early so that people will notice him when he leaves, or who is constantly "name dropping." Such pomposity is always a cloak which covers a terrible fear—the fear that somebody will find out that we are simply very ordinary persons, which indeed we probably are. When we stop role playing and just see ourselves as we are, we will suddenly find that we are relaxed. We will not be trying to convince anyone of anything.

Nearly all exaggerated conduct is overcompensation for repressed inferiority, that terrible fear of being thought or discovered to be inferior. Frank recognition of inferiority does not matter; it is the emotional tone of the complex that is significant. The loss of temper, for example, is an exhibition of overassertiveness and vividly demonstrates one's feelings of inadequacy. Professor David Eitzn, an eminent psychologist, says that such actions as slamming the door, walking too rapidly, stamping on the floor, and unreasonably arguing with our associates are in reality manifestations of our incapability to face and intelligently approach obstacles placed in our way. Whether manifested as moodiness, sulkiness, or as an outburst of temper, the problem is the same sense of inferiority. How many of us have found ourselves losing an argument and inwardly slipping, and so we take to shouting? This is the law of overcompensation at work. We can't win with logic so we will win with sound effects. Touchy people are unsure people. They are looking for slights, for they have a subconscious feeling that they deserve them. You can tell the real size of a man by the size of the things that upset him.

2. *Underassertion* is another false compensation for an inferiority complex. This characteristic is difficult to deal with, because here the individual

asserts his own inferiority and uses it as a kind of foil, a defense mechanism. Some use their sense of inferiority to get recognition and gratification for which their souls crave. Sometimes you meet a man on the golf course who plays very well, but always assumes an air of super modesty. You ask him to play with you and he says, "Well, I don't really play very well; I just can't seem to get my clubs going. I'm just not very good, that's all." And you say, "That's all right, because I don't play too well myself." Once you get out on the golf course he beats the daylights out of you. The queer twist here is that he is egotistical in his assumed humility. The well-adjusted person would say, "Sure, I'll be glad to play," and then will play the best game he can with relaxed naturalness.

Then there is the professor who writes five books on theology and says, "Of course, I'm not a theologian...." The person who constantly depreciates himself enjoys the fact that those who hear him are saying, "Oh, how humble he is! My, what humility!" He gains exactly the compensation desired because of his inferiority complex by acknowledging his inferiority, thus receiving praise for it in the name of humility. A truly humble person never exaggerates the importance of humility, nor does he ever think about it or even realize it.

3. *Infantile regression* is another form of false compensation. The mind, in its inability to face life on an adult level, slips back to childhood outlets. Dr. Leslie Weatherhead tells of a young navy lieutenant on a battleship during World War II who was under great strain. On one occasion, after

an extended, nerve-racking search for submarines over the gray waters of the North Sea, he was found in his cabin playing with a teddy bear. His was a borderline condition and one more serious than the ordinary observer would find in everyday life. But modern life furnishes instances of this same tendency toward the infantile impulse of regression. Anyone in a serious and difficult situation who pouts or feels unduly hurt is exhibiting such a regression because of the failure to act with mature attitudes and behavior.

Consider the man who says he doesn't go to church because he was forced to go when he was a child. This man has not made a mature, specific judgment as to whether the church did or could do him any good or not. But because as a youth he was controlled by a dominating personality, and because it was under that domination that he went to church, he feels that if he does go now he would still be obeying the tyrannical force that controlled him as a child. So, in not going to church, he continues his absurd rebellion. Ironically, by this time, the father who made him attend church has likely been in heaven for thirty years. But the man continues to manifest his immaturity, and he will do so until the day dawns that he learns to judge the church on the basis of the message that it *now* has and the good that it *now* offers, instead of reverting to infantile regression and rebellion against a tyranny that doesn't even exist anymore.

Sometimes an inferiority complex takes a curious turn, and a deep, inner feeling of inadequacy may manifest itself in an unreasonable desire to dominate others. A person who, as a child, was excessively dominated may, as an adult, overcompensate for this by becoming tyrannical in kind. I have seen many instances of a son who was made absolutely miserable by a dominating father, and paradoxically became exactly like him.

4. *The desire for notoriety* is another type of compensation for an inferiority complex. Pathological psychology tells us that people occasionally commit criminal acts just for the sake of the sensation they may cause.

5. Perhaps the saddest of all compensations is that of *fantasy, a flight from reality*. A tragic and dramatic example of this may be seen in the person who identifies so thoroughly with another real or imagined person that in his mind he actually becomes the person he has fantasized. More commonly, a troubled person may create a new and different world environment and value scale in his mind, and thereby escape the problems and responsibilities of the real world about him. The danger of living in a fantasy world as an escape from feelings of inferiority lies in the possibility that the person will eventually lose all touch with reality, slipping from mild neurosis to real psychosis.

6. Another type of false compensation is that of a definite neurosis, that which can often lead to the so-called *nervous breakdown.* It is as though the subconscious mind said to the victim, "This is a good way to hide your inferiority, end your conflicts, and bask in the limelight of sympathy and attention." Certainly there are some people who do this consciously, but there are many for whom

this is a subconscious reaction. I should like, therefore, to speak a word of warning against criticism of the true neurotic. It is as unfair to blame a person for being neurotic as it is to blame him for having the measles.

During World War II many men developed what is called "battle fatigue." Some of them may have been cowards, but the vast majority were actually psychologically ill. It was their subconscious minds that suggested to them this false way of escape. They developed actual physical symptoms to save them from the awful strain of war and the sense of inferiority born of an inability to face it. Such is the path leading to the nervous breakdown, an almost socially acceptable peacetime variety of "battle fatigue." In this way far too many people become ill. "Bromides" have no effect on the subconscious mind, nor can the keenest scalpel dissect it.

The whole question of inferiority—and the only certain way to avoid its many problems—rests in a spiritual solution. God has planted within our personalities certain possibilities, and it is for us to find what these possibilities are and not to waste their tremendous energies by making false compensations that deceive ourselves even more than we deceive the world around us.

To prevent or overcome an inferiority complex you must—

1. *Be absolutely honest with yourself.* Sincerely try to discover the conditions responsible for your feelings of inadequacy, and then by all means try to be an adult. Stop playing the part of a child, and

64

take a long look at Christ. A great many modern cults make the tragic mistake of centering people's energies and attentions upon *self*-cultivation, and they leave behind a multitude of wistful but frustrated people, lifted for a moment but limping for a lifetime. The reason you shouldn't attempt this is that you dare not center yourself upon yourself. If you do, as surely as fate you will lose yourself. Jesus said, "Whosoever shall save his life shall lose it." If you center on your own life, you will "lose" it. As long as Peter had his eyes on Christ, he could defy the elements; he could walk across that surface least likely to be solid, that liquid, crystal pavement of water. But the moment he took his eyes off Christ to consider himself, he was so conditioned to circumstances that they overwhelmed him and down he went. If you look at yourself, or at others, you'll sink. Look at Christ alone, and he will help you to walk on anything!

Someone has suggested that if you say to yourself, "Salivate," the probabilities are that no saliva will come into your mouth. On the contrary, it will probably dry up. But just *begin* to think about a juicy prime rib with mashed potatoes and hot gravy and you won't have any problems salivating. You must not concentrate on yourself, even for the purpose of self-cultivation. Concentrate on Christ and you will be cultivated. The law of losing one's life to find it runs through everything. Jesus said, "Consider the lilies of the field, how they grow..." (Matt. 6:28, KJV). How do they grow? By being self-conscious and fussily trying to grow and look beautiful? No, they look at the sun and in

65

their sun-centeredness they grow to be beautiful.

Occupy yourself with Christ and you will be Christ-like. When we stand face to face with Christ it has a self-revealing effect upon our lives; it is a cleansing experience. The presence of Jesus Christ, unlike the imagined presence of other great men, does not drive us into feelings of inferiority. He sees beneath the worst to the best, and so we can believe in ourselves because we cannot deny his confidence in us. God has faith in us. We are always saying, "We put our faith in him"; likewise, he puts his faith in us, so *much* so that he gave his only begotten Son to live and to die for you and me, while we were yet sinners! His presence in our lives has the power of calling forth everything in us that is splendid. Faint, dull embers begin to blaze again; hope is quickened; life is renewed and becomes exciting. We are reinforced within, and he has the power of utilizing all we ever hope to be, drafting it into his service. His knowledge of us is neither better nor worse than the truth, and piercing to the motive. All he asks is that we should be our very best, surrendered to him. No man who lives in that awareness can ever be victimized by feelings of inferiority.

2. *Appraise what you can and cannot do.* Dr. C. S. Congdon, a psychologist, says that when confronted with a problem or difficult situation, you will use one of four methods to deal with it: flee it, fight it, forget it, or face it. The first three ways will end in failure; only the fourth opens doors. The first step is to face the facts—all the facts. There is all the difference in the world between an

abominable conceit and the man who quietly says to himself, "I know I can do this." Egotism is the anesthetic we may take in order to deaden the pain of feeling inferior. But the sooner we begin to do without the anesthetic and are able to bear the truth, the sooner we awaken to the joy of real living. Let the power in your personality be mobilized. God asks only that you be the best "you" you can be!

3. *Put on a victorious spirit.* Romans 8:31: "If God is on our side, who can ever be against us?" Faith in Christ puts fight into a man so that he develops a terrific resistance to defeat. Obstacles do not alter him; they are merely stepping stones to cross over from failure to victory. Faith and fortitude keep a man going when he seems defeated. If you put your trust in Christ and persevere with unremitting energy and intelligence, you will build such a solid foundation beneath you that you'll mount up on the wings of victory! Therefore, train your mind never to accept the thought of defeat about anything.

What does the New Testament say to the man who has a sense of inferiority? Among other things, it says that all service ranks the same with God. It is not what your daily work is, but the spirit in which you do it. God asks from us that we discover all the resources of our being, mobilize them into activity, and surrender them to his service. If a garbage collector does this, he is serving God as much as the minister of the largest congregation, or the finest surgeon in a great hospital. In the sight of God there is no such thing as menial work. Do your job well, as well as it can be done, in his strength, and utilize every opportunity to magnify the Lord Jesus Christ. This is glorifying God. It is only required in stewards that they be found faithful.

But there is more—the New Testament teaches that Christ is the realization of all our dreams. Whatever we may think of one another, whatever comparisons we may make, our matchless Lord does not think less of a man who has an accent or who eats peas from his knife or whose breath always smells of onions. What he does care about is whether or not we are sincere with ourselves and kind to others. For those who have the Spirit of Christ there is only one test of value, and that is moral character. We must keep our eyes on Christ, who alone can help us keep our sense of values in the right perspective. The Christian has a wonderful way to preclude an inferiority complex. First of all, he asks God that he may have his vision cleared to see himself. When he is ready to look at himself fearlessly, relentlessly, inexorably, then he asks that his sight may be clear in order that he may see the wonderful Christ, for in him he realizes moral values—the only values that count.

Strange miracles happen when you develop a sense of Christ's presence in your life. Though you may be conscious of your own relative insignificance in this huge world, his greatness, far beyond that of the world, is not the kind that pulls you down. It is the kind that stimulates you, inspires you, stirs you, calls you, thrills you, and lifts you higher than you have ever been. Because of his presence and his complete love for us as individuals, he has the amazing power to make you believe in yourself. He makes you utterly humble and at the same time tremendously proud. You are lowered to the dust but exalted to the stars. It is as though the incarnate Christ were saying to you, "This is the 'abundant life' I want so much for you to have." The greatest thing any of us can do is to so live life that it expresses Christ in a way that others see Christ in us. *This* is the cure for feelings of inadequacy and inferiority, to be able to say with all your heart, "I can do all things through Christ, who strengtheneth me." With him the doors of life turn outward instead of inward. Instead of living in the numbing, dooming hell of self-pity, we live in the glory of *his* love, the courage of *his* will, and the success of *his* saving power! Don't ever feel inferior if you belong to Jesus Christ, because you are a *child of the King!*

◆ ◆ ◆

Then he called his disciples and the crowds to come over and listen. "If any of you wants to be my follower," he told them, "you must put aside your own pleasures and shoulder your cross, and follow me closely. If you insist on saving your life, you will lose it. Only those who throw away their lives for my sake and for the sake of the Good News will ever know what it means to really live."
MARK 8:34, 35

For I can do everything God asks me to with the help of Christ who gives me the strength and power.
PHILIPPIANS 4:13

CHAPTER FOUR

The power of faith

It has been said that if we don't have within us that which is above us, we will soon yield to that which is around us. We become conditioned by circumstances, fed on by circumstances, and we grow weak and anemic on the fare, and when we turn within for resources, we find that the well is dry. Life can never be abundant unless it has abundant resources to draw from. A distinguished philosopher once said that in man's search for peace and truth in life, he reaches a certain point and then finds he hasn't the inner resources to complete himself, and so he remains incomplete, unfulfilled, and frustrated. The atheist, unwilling to recognize the most adequate resources from which to draw, has been described as "a man who has no invisible means of support."

In a world where crisis seems so constant, the dictum that love and faith in God could make us whole and sound is a clear call of hope to men and women in despair. Faith means healing, with regard to our spiritual need, and fruition in a physical as well as spiritual sense. The love that has its foundation in faith in the revelation of God has no fear of itself. It is spontaneous and rewarding.

Many people today are finding themselves strangely unhappy in their personal lives because they do not experience the glorious feeling of faith in God. And because they do not have faith in God, they do not have faith in their fellowman. Where there is not the anchor of a perpendicular faith, there is very soon the loss of a horizontal faith. Dr. Blanton said that only when we realize our own limitations can we receive help from outside ourselves. Everyone feels the need of some sustaining power beyond and above himself. Life is too complex, too unpredictable, too difficult, and too severe for us to face with only our own feeble powers and limited discernment.

The words "have faith" are commonly repeated as a cliché. But it is not enough to merely "have faith." What is important is the object of our faith. We place our faith in a physician because of his acquired knowledge and skills. In this same way we cannot exercise a meaningful faith in Jesus Christ until we know who he is and recognize his abilities and credentials that qualify him to meet our needs.

The average man feels vaguely that Christianity has sources of power available to him, but he does not know any workable method for utilizing this power, or for even feeling the magic of its presence in his life. When he is told that through faith in Christ all his troubles can be eliminated and that life can be strong and effective, he is probably skeptical (though wishful) that such marvelous results are possible. Some people have never had anything wonderful happen to them, so they doubt that anything so great *could* happen. They suffer from what a great thinker referred to as "the vast inertia of the soul." But it is a fact that any person's life can be so completely changed that every crippling attitude or habit—whether known or subconscious—that interferes with his well-being can be eliminated or effectively controlled. This is no mere academic assertion, but one that can be fully documented from the experiences of myriads of people in whom these amazing results were obtained.

Faith in Jesus Christ is the answer to the tensions, anxieties, worries, conflicts and complexes that are making millions of lives hell on earth. Dr. William Brown, professor of mental philosophy at Oxford and psychotherapist at King's College Hospital in London, was analyzed for ninety-two hours. Afterwards he said that he found his religious convictions and feelings stronger than ever and that they were purified from sentimental and accidental accompaniments. He came away realizing more than ever before that religious faith is the most important thing in life and the most essential element in mental health.

Often people refer to faith as a commodity, something that may be possessed quantitatively. Some say, "I wish I had your faith," as though it were something you could own and put in a bag. Faith is in reality a form of action; it is something you exercise. In the New Testament, faith is explicit trust in a Person—the Lord Jesus Christ.

72

There is a great difference between saying, "Every day in every way I am getting better and better," and "My faith is in the Lord Jesus Christ," for here your faith is in a Person, *the* Person who brought God to us in terms we could understand—God in corporeality, God in human form, God so that we can know and love him—further, God in a great redemptive purpose. How wonderful to be able to say, "In him who strengtheneth me, I am ready for *anything*!"

"Have faith," says the psychologist who does not know Christ; but that is not enough; it won't work. I should have a Person who can take my broken life and unify it, help me harness my wild impulses to his plan and transfer my problems to his care and keeping. The most skillful analyst cannot reach the deepest area of my need. Only Christ—the incarnate God—can fill the vacuum in my soul.

Our Lord put great emphasis on the necessity of having faith. He rebuked men because they had such little faith. He was constantly saying to his disciples, "Oh, ye of little faith!" In his picturesque way he told them that if they only had faith as a grain of mustard seed they could move mountains. Apparently even his own mighty works depended upon *their faith* in many instances (Mark 11:23, 24). In his home town of Nazareth there were no miracles because of unbelief (Matt. 13:58).

The Apostle Paul emphasized the necessity of this trusting faith. He said we are saved "through faith," that we are justified "by faith." The author of The Epistle to the Hebrews puts faith in a place of prime importance: "What is faith? It is the confident assurance that something we want is going to happen. It is the certainty that what we hope for is waiting for us, even though we cannot see it up ahead" (Heb. 11:1). The book of James commends the fact that it is by *faith* that men are to be healed: "... the prayer of faith shall save the sick..." (James 5:15, KJV).

It would seem, then, a question of great importance to ask what faith is, and how, in this particular century, we may be expected to exercise it. The faith a scientist demonstrates is not a projection from fantasy, but from all he already knows, has tried and proved. Similarly, for the Christian, faith is a projection from all that he knows and has learned from all possible reliable sources of knowing. In this respect, theology is a necessity. The organizing and cataloging of spiritual truths by great Christian scholars, the study of the Word of God synthetically, analytically, and expositionally, with a desire to make the application of its truths coalesce with life, the verification of the Scriptures by the study of Christian evidence, geography, archaeology, history, prophecy, etc., the experience of the saints through the ages, and the illumination of the Holy Spirit all help to lay down a firm road to the place from which the step of faith can best be taken.

The mathematician uses faith. One of the romances of astronomy was the discovery of the planet Neptune through a leap of faith. Proceeding along the road of tested, scientific truth, astronomers found that at one point in its vast circuit through the heavens, the planet Uranus (which revolves around the sun every eighty-four years) swung out of its normal curve. What was it that attracted that vast planet and caused it to alter its course? From the deviation of Uranus mathematicians actually calculated the distance, direction and weight of the disturbing body. Its orbit was calculated even before the planet itself had been seen. Then, with a glorious leap of faith, astronomers swept their telescopes across the night sky and found Neptune, one of the outermost planets of the solar system, 2,794 million miles from the sun, and with a period of revolution of over 160 years.

In a similar category of events, but far more inspiring and amazing, was the deviation in the moral course of human life, when God spoke in his revelatory truth and invaded the stream of human history in the incarnation. This discovery also requires a step of faith—the belief that God has indeed revealed himself in the written Word and in the Person of Jesus Christ.

Faith, then, can be defined as the projection of the mind from what it can definitely prove toward that which is intuitively discerned. Christian faith is the projection of mind and heart from what is already known and tested toward that which, in response to inward experience and vision, is spiritually apprehended. Faith is believing that God is there, that he has spoken in his Word and in his Son. Faith in the living Christ is saving faith whereby we receive him, trust him, rest upon him, commit ourselves utterly and totally to him and to

75

him alone for the salvation he offers us in the gospel. As the writer of Hebrews says, "We are confident that something we want is going to happen, and certain that what we hope for is waiting for us, even though we cannot see it up ahead" (Heb. 11:1†).

The possibility of faith is never reduced by knowledge. On the contrary, it is enhanced and increased by it. This to me is one of the most unique and exciting characteristics of Christian revelation. For example, let the specialist in biology give even a fraction of the time spent on his favorite subject to an in-depth study of Christian evidence, or apologetics, and then of the Scriptures and the evidence concerning the Person and claims of Jesus Christ. If he is sincere and absolutely honest, he will be convinced that Christianity is no wild dream of uneducated fanatics but is based as much on living truth as any of the sciences. In fact, the original autographs, the biblical documents of both the Old and the New Testaments, possess an integrity, authenticity, and reliability not to be found in any other ancient document. Converted skeptics such as Sir William Ramsey, the archaeologist, Frank Morrison, the English journalist, C. S. Lewis, the British author, Lew Wallace, the novelist, and a host of others actually set out to disprove the validity of the Christian faith. After examining the evidence they came to subscribe to the Christian faith with such allegiance that they became its champions.

It is the idea of some that Christianity is irrational. But I believe that the Christian is the *true* rationalist, for he will attend to all the aspects of truth. All truth can be built into his fabric and become part of the road that leads to an even greater confidence in revelation. Occasionally it is said that faith has nothing to do with knowledge, that it is "intellectual suicide," a gigantic plunge one takes and hopes there's something there. Nothing could be more misleading. True faith is a leap from the known to the unknown, but it is *based* on the known. Let the seeker, therefore, gather all the knowledge he can to make his road toward the final bridge of faith. Let him examine what the great theologians have learned from their correlation and organizing of the truths obtained from the Word of God. Let him give himself to a systematic, intensive study of the testimony of Scripture itself. Let him consider the evaluation of all the corroborative evidence found in Christian apologetics. Let him weigh the evidence from what the saints experienced in the record of their lives as found in the Word of God, and the evidence that consists in the survey of lives that are being changed today within the realm of our own experience through the penetrating power of our Lord Jesus Christ.

To put it succinctly, we believe that God has revealed himself. Revelation consists of truth man could never acquire, reason out, learn from experience, or know on his own—apart from God's revealing it to him. God has revealed himself in the written Word, the Bible, and in the living Word, Jesus Christ. The Bible, unlike any other religious book in the world, can be reasonably authenticated on the basis of geography, history, archaeology, and the fulfillment of prophecy. And, as Einstein might speak on relativity, so Jesus Christ is the only authority when it comes to spiritual matters. Thus, it will be the utter trust in the words of Christ that will bring the great victory of confident faith.

In the art of exercising faith as a working principle of life, there is first of all a prerequisite: the study of God's Word with the desire to coalesce your life with its truth in obedience. By this I mean a deeper knowledge of God and of the revelation of himself in Jesus Christ as the apostle expressed it, "... that I may know him ..." (Phil. 3:10, KJV). In John 6:28 it is recorded that Jews came to our Lord and said to him, "What should we do, to satisfy God?" Jesus answered, "This is the will of God, that you believe in the one he has sent" (John 6:29). In knowing him, they would know God. What a tremendous fact! He said, "Anyone who has seen me has seen the Father ..." (John 14:9). "I and my Father are one" (John 10:30). "I am the way the truth, and the life ..." (John 14:6, KJV). Hebrews 11:6 tells us, "You can never please God without faith, without depending on him. Anyone who wants to come to God must believe that there is a God and that he rewards those who sincerely look for him." As Pascal put it: Faith is betting your life on God!

The late Henry Drummond was one of the superior intellects and scholars of his time. Beyond this he was a spiritual genius, one of those rare characters who gain acute insight into spiritual laws. Drummond's secret was so simple that anyone can put it into practice: Ten minutes spent in Christ's presence every day—even two minutes—will make the whole day different. Multiply those few minutes a day by every day and add the culminating effect of habit and the changed mental outlook, and you will understand how this brief period, faithfully observed, can change everything—your entire *life*.

An elderly blind Indian in the West, a magnificent person of inner peace and kindly spirit, revealed the source of his strength when he said that it is easy to believe in God when you live alone with him in the dark. He knew what it was to exercise a meaningful faith, because spiritually he *lived with* God. Time spent in the Word of God, allowing its truths by the Holy Spirit to search our lives, and time spent with the Lord Jesus Christ in the confession of weakness, sin, and failure, and prayer for those who have wronged you, asking strength and courage to live consistently and triumphantly, will ultimately bring a day when faith as a principle of life will bring power to your personality that you cannot even imagine and of which you may possibly not even be aware! The Holy Spirit will literally take over your life and the inflammatory touch of Christ's compassion will consume your heart.

Dr. Norman Vincent Peale tells of a Chinese gentleman, a successful broker, who gave his testimony. He came from a wealthy family and had every opportunity that wealth and social connections could afford. However, he ultimately lost his wife through dissipation and the bulk of his wealth through gambling. His health failed, and a nervous breakdown rendered him fit for only very limited activity. At this juncture he met some people whose joy and delight in life amazed him. It awakened in him a hope that there might be a way out of his sad failure. They told him there was a way and that all he need do was have faith in Christ. But the advice was futile. *Faith* was something he just did not have—neither in God, his fellowman, nor himself. But he was one of those rare souls who, once being convinced of great possibilities, is not daunted by an obstacle however formidable. Evidently he had no problem with respect to the infallibility and the authority of Scripture, nor with regard to deity of Jesus Christ. But "faith" had never become a working principle in his life.

He began a daily plan of communication with God on the advice of a wise friend who advised him that this was the sure method of gaining faith and confidence. During his time spent in the Word of God and in prayer he would ask himself four questions:

1. What have I to thank God for in the last twenty-four hours?
2. What sins have I committed in the last twenty-four hours?
3. What does God want me to do?
4. Whom should I pray for?

The time period of the first two questions he limited to twenty-four hours because the memory is often inclined not to be reliable unless the period of analysis is short. He said that he began to find resources he never knew were there, and somehow what were mere words on pages were translated into actual life patterns, and he gradually overcame his disability. His mind began to function with its old efficiency, and today he is a radiantly happy man, whose life is centered on Jesus Christ. Many years ago this was called "practicing the presence of Christ." And indeed we are bidden to do exactly that today. Never for a moment of the day or an hour of the night must we lose the consciousness of his wonderful presence! "Yet faith comes from listening to this Good News—the Good News about Christ" (Rom. 10:17).

The second and ultimate method for exercising meaningful faith is by surrendering your life absolutely, entirely, and forever to Jesus Christ. In that moment of commitment we are told that the Holy Spirit comes to dwell in the believer. 1 Corinthians 6:19: "Haven't you yet learned that your body is the home of the Holy Spirit God gave you, and that he lives within you? Your own body does not belong to you." See to it that nothing is allowed to jeopardize the sovereignty of Christ upon the throne of your heart!

The Word of God says, "According to your faith be it unto you" (Matt. 9:29). That is to say, we *receive* in direct proportion to the amount of faith we exercise. The prayer of the man with the demon-possessed son—"I do have faith; oh, help me to have *more*!" (Mark 9:24)—is the attitude that opens the door to a new life. It is saying, "I trust you, Lord; I believe even though shadowy questions haunt my mind." The spirit struggles to believe, to triumph over the weak doubtings of the earthbound body. The release of power that comes with this victory of faith is the most impressive phenomenon of human experience.

This total surrender to Christ also involves the giving up of certain things in your life. Anything that constitutes sin of any kind or degree, whether gross sins of the flesh or the more subtle sins of the disposition, must immediately be put out of your life. Many so-called Christians might not inappropriately be termed "segment Christians"; the Holy Spirit indwells them, but he is not permitted absolute sovereignty. This describes the carnal Christian—miserable, ineffective, shorn of power. Our Lord said, "For anyone who keeps his life for himself shall lose it; and anyone who loses his life for me shall find it again. What profit is there if you gain the whole world—and lose eternal life? What can be compared with the value of eternal life?" (Matt. 16:25, 26). In other words, the total abandonment of self to Christ is the beginning of the true life of faith.

The Apostle Paul commands us, "... give your bodies to God. Let them be a living sacrifice, holy—the kind he can accept. When you think of what he has done for you, is this too much to ask?" (Rom. 12:1). In other words, we are to place our bodies at the disposal of God. Then he adds, "And be not conformed to this world [stop masquerading in the habiliments of the world's mannerisms, styles and habits], but be ye transformed by the renewing of your mind, that ye may prove what is that good, and acceptable, and perfect will of God [so that what you reflect is what you really are]" (Rom. 12:2, KJV). Here he is saying that we are not only to surrender our bodies, but we are to surrender the innermost recesses of our beings to God. This surrender must be a total surrender. It also means that we are to put something *into* our life—an ever-growing consciousness of the presence and power of the Holy Spirit. Great resources are available to the person who learns to trust God completely, to rest utterly his life, with all its problems and burdens, on the God who is there. So often we mumble a few creeds, we live more or less respectable lives and we think we are people of faith, which we are not. Often we are starving to death spiritually.

Real faith is inevitably associated with lives of power, effectiveness, and usefulness. For me to float successfully on water necessitates a belief that the water will hold me up, or I will not even attempt it at all. Even so, there must be a similar surrender to God. We must rest in that absolute confidence that underneath are the everlasting arms, that we can do all things through Christ, who strengthens and upholds us. When we can actually say that our lives are "hidden with Christ in God," then we will experience the strength, the inner peace, and the sense of being attached to the very power of God, so that no matter what life may bring in the way of exigency, emergency or even grim tragedy, we can confidently have "overwhelming victory ... through Christ who loved us enough to die for us" (Rom. 8:37). Such is the victory of faith in Christ. The more faith grows, the more it is directed—not toward things, even worthy things, but toward Christ.

An English preacher once said that the more faith grows, the less it strives or cries. It makes the communion of the soul with God its first quest, whether gifts, such as health, follow or not. One of the loveliest illustrations of this is found in the 23rd Psalm. In it we find no agonizing cry to God to give this or do that. Quietly, in marvelous language, poetic insight, spiritual apprehension, and in the *present tense,* the soul asserts to itself that its needs *are being fulfilled.* It is not "O Lord, *be* my shepherd," but "The Lord *is* my shepherd; I shall not want. He *is* making me to lie down in green pastures; he *is* leading me beside the still waters. He *is* restoring my soul; he *is* leading me in the paths of righteousness for his name's sake."

The miracle of Christianity, a miracle that far outsoars even the miracles of the days of our Lord's ministry on earth, is the present offer and the realization of such a relationship with the living Christ. Through all the ages he offers himself to every person. Let your faith see that vision in front of you; let the eye of the soul be captivated by it. Let the mind paint a picture of a personality always in touch with that radiant presence and itself dwelling in communion with Christ, which becomes even richer and deeper. Then, according to our faith, it shall be done unto us. To dwell with that presence is to be increasingly transformed— regardless of what happens to our body, for it is a

84

transforming friendship, the greatest regenerating influence the world has ever known. In that deeper knowledge of Jesus Christ and the total surrender of your life to him, God will become real, and the principle of faith will become as effective in your life as it was in the lives of those who are cited in that magnificent roll call found in the 11th chapter of Hebrews. But the necessity of childlike faith can never be overstressed. Our Lord said time and time again, "Except ye become as little children, ye shall not enter into the kingdom of heaven."

For many people the idea of God is a great abstraction, a philosophical idea. It is impossible for us to conceive of a cosmic intelligence that fills the infinitude of endless space. But in Jesus Christ, God becomes real; he is brought into the realm of our experiences in a way that we can see him, know him, love him, and live with him every day of our lives.

This has been beautifully illustrated in the story of an elderly Scotsman who was very ill. His minister called to see him, and the old man directed the minister's attention to a vacant chair beside his bed. He explained its presence by saying that in his early years he had found it difficult to pray, often falling asleep on his knees because he was so tired after the day's labors. He said that even if he was able to stay awake it was often with great difficulty that he kept his thoughts from wandering. He became worried about it and spoke to the man then his pastor, who said, "Don't think that you must kneel down to pray; just sit down and put a chair opposite you and imagine that Jesus is in it, then talk to him as you would to a long time friend." The Scotsman continued that he had been doing that ever since, and that it had worked.

A week later the daughter of the old Scotsman drove up to the minister's house. When she was shown into his study, she sobbed, "Father died in the night. I had no idea that death could be so near. I had just gone to lie down for an hour or so. He seemed to be sleeping so comfortably, but when I went back he was dead. He hadn't moved since I saw him, except that his hand was on that empty chair by the side of the bed. Isn't that strange?"

"No," said the minister, "it isn't so strange." He understood. Then he told her of her father's great secret. He had made God an actual factor in his daily life, and by living with him in that way, he had found that it was not a process of imagination, as some might declare it to be, but that God, through Christ, over the years had become an increasingly real Person to him.

We read in Hebrews 11:6, "You can never please God without faith, without depending on him. Anyone who wants to come to God must believe that there is a God and that he rewards those who sincerely look for him." The practice of a systematic devotional life that causes you to grow in grace and in the knowledge of Christ, a total surrender of your life to Jesus Christ and a daily surrender, will ultimately make Jesus Christ real in your life. There is for our benefit in the Christian faith a greater power than we ever knew existed. By faith the power of God can be released into human experience on a day to day, moment by moment basis. Spiritual equipment for successful conquest was promised by our Lord when he said, "But when the Holy Spirit has come upon you, you will receive power ..." (Acts 1:8).

◆ ◆ ◆

For every child of God
can obey him, defeating sin and evil pleasure by
trusting Christ to help him.
1 JOHN 5:4

CHAPTER FIVE

Freedom from fear and anxiety

It has been said that fear, in the form of unrelieved anxiety, is the official emotion of our age. It is the most pervasive psychological phenomenon of our time, fully understood by no one, and the central problem in understanding and treating mental illness. Such is the opinion of prominent psychologists and psychiatrists today. Some have suggested that we are living in an age of such profound anxiety or fear that it has become a universal emotion. In the *Encyclopedia of Mental Health,* J. Marmor concludes that the twentieth century is more anxiety-ridden than any other era in history since the Middle Ages. Gary R. Collins, in his book *A Psychologist Looks at Life,* states that modern technology is producing such rapid and far-reaching changes in our standard of living that people are becoming anxious simply trying to keep up with it! In addition, mass media has made it possible to be immediately aware of local and national problems. The tensions of the middle and far East, our troubled economy, exploding campuses, pollution, over-population, hunger, tension and inequity in the ghettos, crime and civil disobedience, the increasing ability of scientists to manipulate and control human behavior, the changing values of youth, and a host of other issues are constantly bombarding us. Is it any wonder that modern man experiences anxiety?

Fear, in the form of anxiety, however, is usually much more personal in scope and cause. It is the emotion we feel whenever we face anything that seems to be threatening, whether a situation or an object. It is characterized by sensations of apprehension, dread, uneasiness, worry or concern, often accompanied by physiological reactions—increased pulse rate, perspiration flow, etc., depending upon our particular response to the situation. Apprehension, anxiety and fear can spring from a thousand sources, from imagined danger to actual peril, from concern about embarrassment to undiagnosed illness.

Psychological studies show that the resultant feeling can vary widely. Anxiety can be either specific or free floating. Specific anxieties result when we are consciously aware of some threatening situation or object. Claustrophobia, for example, is a specific anxiety that arises because one has a fear of being in a closed situation. Others feel anxious about height, traveling over water, the presence of snakes, etc. (In all, there are 645 classifications of phobia.)

The second kind of anxiety is the *free floating* type. Here the person does not know why he feels as he does. He is afraid something terrible is going to happen, but what it is or what he can do about it is a mystery to him.

Fearful anxiety can also be either acute or chronic. An acute condition is one that comes quickly, is of high intensity and of short duration, as acute appendicitis. A chronic condition is usually of lower intensity but lasts for a much longer time, as a chronic heart condition.

Dr. Collins suggests four reasons why people become anxious: First, we learn by experience to be anxious, as was demonstrated by Pavlov's dogs. We can be conditioned to feel anxious and to fear. When a person takes a test and fails, he associates the pain of failure with the test situation. The next time he takes a test, he is *anxious* because of what he has learned through the past experience.

A second cause of anxiety is the example shown by other people. Children learn to be anxious by watching reactions of parents and other adults. The mother who is anxious during a thunderstorm, for example, conveys anxiety to the child who later becomes anxious in the same situation.

A third cause is "socialization," the process by which a child learns and adopts the standards and customs of his particular culture. From almost the first day of birth, parents, and later teachers and other adults, place limitations on a child and establish rules so that the young person will know exactly how to behave in a given circumstance. To assure this conformity, adults reward the child's behavior when it is desirable, withhold something he wants when the behavior is unacceptable, and punish undesirable behavior. The child is also threatened. "Misbehave," we say, "and you will be spanked," or sent to your room, not permitted to have your dessert, or deprived in some other way. These threats help mold the child, but they also teach him to be anxious. Anxiety, therefore, is unfortunately taught along with the rules of society.

Fourth, anxiety comes as we learn to *think*. A little child wanders into a busy street without fear because he has not yet learned to understand the danger of fast-moving automobiles. Parents may watch television and learn of civil strife, economic tensions in the society, and the energy crisis, while the child plays happily on the floor, because he has not yet learned to understand the meaning of the newscaster's words.

Panic, an extreme form of anxiety, is felt only when trapped people realize the danger of a situation, recognize the importance of escaping, and the difficulty of getting out. Also, once we learn what is right and wrong we can comprehend the implications of our actions. This may cause us to become anxious when we are tempted to sin, or anxious after we have sinned, since we then are faced with our own frailties and the threat of punishment. This anxiety over morals is at the basis of much guilt.

Another cause of anxiety has been proposed by Sigmund Freud. If we consciously think about all that could harm us or adversely influence our society, we would become immobilized with fear and insecurity. To prevent this, our brain manages to ignore a lot of the potential stresses and automatically pushes these "out of our minds" and into what Freud calls the *unconscious*. Thus, many of our concerns and threats get lodged somewhere in the brain where we don't consciously think about them. The anxiety-arousing issues and the realizations of potential dangers are still present, but we don't ponder these consciously. At times, however, they still produce anxiety of a free floating type, caused not by conscious thinking but by subconscious influences.

As Christians, how are we to cope with anxiety and fear? Our Lord was always saying that without faith life collapses, but with faith we can move mountains. We can do anything with ourselves and others. Therefore, he was always asking men to throw aside fear and anxiety and take faith. In the midst of a world filled with fears he was constantly saying to all classes of people, "Fear not; only believe."

Anxiety, or fear, in its right place, is a good thing. It is an emotion native to personality, and because of this it must be good, for nothing essentially evil has been planted in our personality by the hand of God. When we say, "The man is fearless," we really mean that he can overcome his fears. If he were literally "fearless," that is, without fear, he could have no courage. Fear is a good thing, for without it there could be no such thing as courage, confidence, or reverence for God.

It is frequently asserted that fear is destructive, which is not entirely true. When one fears something that truly threatens security, it is a protective response. But when fear is incorrectly assessed and directed, it is debilitating and destructive. Freud was the first to make a distinction between normal and neurotic anxiety. Normal anxiety occurs when there is real danger, when it makes sense to be anxious. When the astronauts on the Apollo 12 moon journey had trouble with their space ship and were in danger of being lost in space, apprehension was quite natural and normal. On the other hand, neurotic, abnormal anxiety involves intense feelings of discomfort when danger is mild or even nonexistent. It is not always easy to distinguish between neurotic and normal anxiety—even Freud recognized this—and sometimes it all depends on whose point of view you are taking. For example, you may fly with someone who boasts that he is an excellent pilot, and yet you may sense in him an inherent carelessness, and you immediately feel threatened and uncomfortable. Up to a certain point, fear on the part of a surgeon may make him more skillful and careful lest he cut in the wrong places. But fear pushed beyond a certain point could paralyze him. Every worthwhile accomplishment has an element of healthy fear, which gives us skill and careful drive.

It was a wise man indeed who said, "The fear of the Lord is the beginning of wisdom" (Ps. 111:10, KJV). When we remember the background of the writer of that Psalm and that his theology always linked righteousness with success and disobedience with disaster, we might well paraphrase the sentence—"The fear of consequence is the beginning of wisdom." Fear is legitimate when it is exercised in the interest of the soul. But there is an unhealthy fear that takes away both skill and drive, that inhibits us.

Fulton Sheen has said that modern anxiety is different from the anxiety of previous and more "normal" ages in two ways. In other days men were anxious about their souls, but modern anxiety is principally concerned with the body. To read modern advertisements one would think that the greatest calamity that could befall a human being would be to have dish-pan hands or unpleasant breath. Commercial advertising is "gray" with outright lies and false claims and for the most part is an insult to even the lowest level of intelligence. There is a continual overemphasis of corporal, collective security, and it is not healthy because it instills anxiety and morbid fears.

A distinguished physician once said, "The commonest and the subtlest of all human diseases is fear." Psychologists declare it is the most disintegrating enemy of human personality. Obviously, these scientific men are referring to neurotic anxiety, abnormal fear, and it is indeed a dreadful enemy. Normal anxiety causes the pharmacist to dispense a prescription with care and accuracy; neurotic anxiety would make him run down the street after the customer to get the bottle back for fear that he might have put in arsenic instead of aniseed. Normal anxiety makes the explorer light his fire and leave his revolver loaded when he settles down for the night; neurotic or morbid anxiety would keep him awake all night, eyes wide open, with his gun in his hand. Fear makes a man who is in charge of a leper colony wash his hands and take precautions against infection; morbid fear would send him home on the next plane.

Psychosomatic medicine is teaching us that anxiety, whether normal or neurotic, actually causes diseases. There are immediate physical responses to anxiety. These include changes in blood pressure, the slowing of digestive processes, general tension or changes in the chemical composition of the blood. It is possible under certain circumstances for a person's hair to stand on end, for "goose bumps" to develop on the skin, or for the person to blanch with fear. These physical reactions harm us only if they persist. When this happens the body eventually yields under the pressure. Stomach ulcers, intense headaches, high blood pressure and other physical ailments often occur as a direct result of persistent, unrelieved anxiety or fear. Some say as high as eighty-five percent of our known organic diseases originate in wrong emotions. Dr. Felix Cunha says that incidents of stomach ulcers go up and down with the stock market. The Blumenthal Headache Clinic reports that in every national crisis, headaches increase. Investigation shows that when the Dow Jones averages on the stock market skid down, the number of calls to physicians from businessmen with an upset stomach goes up. Anxiety brings about an overacidity of the stomach, thereby upsetting the digestive tract. Hydrochloric acid pours into the stomach even during sleep. Evidently Solomon saw the connection between anxiety and disease when he wrote, "Banish all your worries from your mind and keep your body free from pain" (Eccl. 11:10†).

The incident is related of a doctor who diagnosed two patients on the same day. One was pronounced seriously ill with only a slight chance of recovery. The other had nothing seriously wrong and would recover. The two diagnoses were written out but by mistake put in the wrong envelopes. The man with only a slight hope recovered, while the man who had little wrong with him died.

Immediately following the great depression of 1929, deaths from gastric ulcers increased 25 percent. An outstanding physician, who had a heart affliction, used to say that his life was in the hands of any man who made him angry. He was right. Anxiety expressed in anger would immediately produce angina pectoris, precipitating his death. Dr. Alexis Carrell, in *Man the Unknown*, reminds us that hate, anger, and fear are capable of bringing confusion even to logic. When habitual, these sentiments are capable of effecting organic changes, resulting in genuine diseases.

Normal anxiety is motivating, but neurotic anxiety destroys efficiency. Frequently it paralyzes an individual and becomes one of the greatest obstacles to a full development of personality and the achievement of success in life. A study of surgical patients by psychologist Irving Janis, in which he divided them into three groups—the non-anxious, the moderately anxious, and the highly anxious— demonstrated that the moderately, or sensibly anxious patient showed the quickest recovery and the best postoperative morale.

This brings us to the remedy—how to overcome neurotic anxiety, or morbid, abnormal fear. Automatically and often without consciously thinking about it, we behave in ways that enable us to deal with our anxiety and to protect ourselves against it. Dr. Collins states that many cope with anxiety by making a joke of it, others by talking over the problem with someone else. Many find a certain amount of relief in emotionalizing their problems by crying. Others forget their anxiety temporarily by sleeping, daydreaming, gorging themselves with food, drowning their anxieties in alcohol, alleviating some of the pressure by taking drugs, or deliberately thinking about something other than the anxiety-producing situation. In recent years chemical techniques have been used for lowering anxiety levels. We have today a broad spectrum of tranquilizers and other medications that can accomplish this.

But the Christian has a different prescription. Dr. Peale tells of a young doctor who in boyhood developed a fear psychosis which grew upon him over the years. By the time he entered medical school it was draining his mental energies to such an extent that it was only by a Herculean effort that he was able to do his work. Nevertheless, he finally graduated and went into internship; but he was still carrying this heavy burden of fear. One day, unable to stand it any longer, he consulted one of his professors and confessed, "I must be rid of this terrible burden of fear or I will have to give up medicine." The older physician, a wise and kindly man, directed the student to a Healer who, as he cleverly said, "keeps office in the New Testament." The young man followed his suggestion and went to that Physician who gave him medicine which made him well. But this medicine was not a liquid in a bottle, nor was it compounded as a pellet; it was in the form of words. It was that potent combination found in 2 Timothy 1:7, (KJV): "For God hath not given us the spirit of fear, but of power, and of love, and of a sound mind." The young physician took these words and allowed them to sink deeply into his mind by a process of intellectual and spiritual osmosis. Their healing potency penetrated and infiltrated his mind and in due course deliverance came, followed by a strange and wonderful sense of peace.

Our Lord advocated this very practice. He said, "If ye abide in me, and my words abide in you, ye shall ask what ye will, and it shall be done unto you" (John 15:7, KJV). If a person "abides," that is, maintains a long-term, habitual mental immersion in communion with Christ and allows his words to linger as permanent thoughts in his mind until the heart is affected, he will develop such a potentiality of power that life will flow *toward* him rather than *away* from him. He will be released and his powers will function efficiently. Law then will operate in his favor rather than against him, for now his changed thought pattern has put him in harmony with law or truth. The Apostle Paul demonstrated this when he said, "But none of these things move me, neither count I my life as dear unto myself ..." (Acts 20:24), and when he declared, "I am ready, not to be bound only but also to die at Jerusalem for the name of the Lord Jesus" (Acts 21:13).

The first factor, then, in overcoming morbid fear is in the word "power." The only power that can counteract neurotic anxiety is the "power of faith." By this I mean such a personal commitment and confidence in the living Christ, that we are willing to look our fears squarely in the face.

A large part of the campaign against anxiety is to get a complete and thoroughgoing knowledge of what that particular anxiety is—not what it *seems* to be, but what it really *is*. The reason fears are apparently so difficult to defeat is that we allow them to remain vague and shadowy. They slip into the subconscious and become real problems. Like any object in the semi-darkness, they assume grotesque shapes and appear larger in size and therefore more formidable than they actually are. Bring them out into the light of day and more often than not, they will shrivel up.

Have you ever been alone at night, possibly in a remote place, and heard a noise outside as though someone were trying to get in the door, and the more you developed fear the more your imagination played havoc, until in desperation you faced the fear by going out to see who the intruder was, only to find that a dog had wandered into your yard and was exploring your garbage can? The moment you opened the door and saw the dog, your fears fled. Many of our fears develop precisely in that manner, and phobias entirely so. A

99

young army pilot became a victim of morbid fear. Through analysis and counseling it was discovered that the source of his fear was that a spider would drop in his mouth while he was asleep, because he always slept with his mouth open. Facing our anxieties reduces them to their legitimate size, and it is true that the worst fear is fear itself.

Our Lord Jesus Chist has met and defeated every anxiety or fear we could ever know. This confidence is our starting point. Nothing can touch us that has not touched him and been defeated by him. The Word of God tells us he was "... touched with the feelings of our infirmities ... tempted [put under stress] like as we are, yet without sin" (Heb. 4:15, KJV). If you open your life to a recognition of his personal presence and power, *every* problem can be defeated. We have the promise "... there is someone in your hearts who is stronger than any evil teacher in this wicked world" (1 John 4:4). We need not be defeated by anything unless we consent to be. In a real dependence upon the Lord Jesus Christ we are caught up in a victory that nothing can restrain except our own refusal to cooperate.

One of the glorious characteristics of the early Christians was a seeming lack of unhealthy or morbid fear; they were afraid of nothing. The apostle could say, "I do not frustrate the grace of God" (Gal. 2:21, KJV). He was a matchless example of Christian triumph. He declared, in Philippians 4:13, "For I can do everything God asks me to with the help of Christ who gives me the strength and power." When Jesus Christ indwells your life in the Person of the Holy Spirit, he can give you power to meet any situation and overcome it.

A paratrooper said, "The first time I jumped from a plane, everything in me resisted. All there was between me and death was a piece of cord and a little patch of silk. But when I actually found out for myself that the patch of silk would hold me, I had the most marvelous feeling of exaltation in all my life! I wasn't afraid of anything and the release from fear filled me with exquisite delight. In fact, I was so happy I did not want to come down." Fear may defeat us if we are unwilling to put our trust in what we unfortunately regard as an ethereal thing, namely, faith in God. But, like the paratrooper, when we leap out, explicitly trusting our matchless Christ, we discover that this confidence sustains us. Furthermore, it is exhilarating!

The second factor in defeating unhealthy fear is *love*. Love is the natural, native, basic relationship that a human being should have with God through the mediation of Jesus Christ. Our text says, "Love contains no fear; indeed, fully developed love expels every particle of fear, for fear always contains some of the torture of feeling guilty. This means that the man who lives in fear has not yet had his love perfected" (1 John 4:18, Moffatt). When we fully realize how enveloped we are in the love of Christ, we can move through this world unafraid, and the only anxieties we experience are legitimate ones.

Henry J. Taylor, the journalist, economist and author of many books, including *Men in Motion,* relates that when he was a little boy he took a trip down into a coal mine with his father. It was during that trip that he discovered for the first time what God is really like. He said it was one of the most vivid experiences of his childhood. In those days there were no elevators; the descent was made in a barrel. He told of his feelings as he climbed into the barrel and descended into the depths of the mine. All during the time the barrel was being lowered he clung to his father in the security that he found there. Later, walking through the dark tunnel of that underground world, one of the miners said to him, "Aren't you afraid?"

He replied, "Well, I'd be awfully scared except my father is with me."

Henry Taylor said that he remembered his father looking at him with a smile and saying, "Then you'll never be afraid, son, because a greater Father than I will always be with you."

Let your fears go; give them to God. The Psalmist said, "When I am afraid, I will trust in thee" (Ps. 56:3, KJV). Have you ever carried a tired child in your arms? Feeling the trust of the child, you hold the little form even closer and with greater care, for you cannot fail such complete confidence. How much more profoundly does God take to his heart all of us who are tired and worn in the dark nights of this life. He said, "Come to me and I will give you rest—all of you who work so hard beneath a heavy yoke" (Matt. 11:28). Surrender your anxieties into the hands of God; turn them over to him. Anxiety results from keeping things in our own hands. When you live in the constant consciousness of the companionship of Jesus Christ, you become courageous, and your life victorious!

Samuel Rutherford, in the dark days of religious tyranny in Scotland, sturdily remarked that he had learned in ill weather to go to the lee side of Christ. He put Christ between him and the storm, and he walked "on the sunny side of the brae." This is the simple secret that committed Christians have discovered to be indispensable to their happiness, well-being, and effectiveness. A Christian saturates his mind with such truths as "The Lord is my shepherd...." He has learned not to let his heart be troubled for he believes in God, and because he *believes* in God he *loves* God and accordingly has fallen upon the sublime truth that "perfect love casteth out fear." Anyone who lives in the literature and the spirit of the New Testament will acquire after awhile a quiet confidence that nothing can shake. Start every day with the affirmation, "Christ is with me, he loves me, I can trust him, so I will do my best and will not be afraid."

Another factor in the defeat of anxiety is found in the words "a sound mind"—a well-balanced mind—and disciplined self-control. Sin, in reality, is a wound in the mind. It is a foreign substance that invades the mind and soul, and the mind tries to close around it but it cannot, and so it becomes infected. If you were to open a fine watch and push a pebble into the works, people would think you were demented. Yet, people do equally destructive things to their minds. Many who suffer ever-deepening anxiety have discovered that the basic cause of their fear is that they have departed from moral living, and have begun to live in disobedience to the Word of God. They have become victims of a sense of unrelieved guilt, because they cannot get away with it. Galatians 6:7 is inexorably true: "A man will always reap just the kind of crop he sows!" The end result of such a tangle of emotional reactions is an "unsound mind."

There is the fear of being found out, the fear of the future, the loss of confidence in yourself. You can become a victim of blind, unreasoning, fundamental fear. Frequently a psychosis develops. Deliverance from such fear can be found through the discipline of Christian morality and by yielding to a life in the control of the Holy Spirit. For when Christ makes you free, "ye shall be free indeed." Follow any other line and you will indeed be found to be unsound, unstable, and eventually irrational.

One way to prevent unhealthy anxiety is to pursue healthy anxiety. Our Lord mentioned at least seven things about which we should never experience anxiety:

1. Having our body killed (Matt. 10:28)
2. What we shall say in the day of persecution when we are called on the carpet before the commissar (Mark 13:11)
3. Whether we should build another barn or skyscraper (parable of the rich fool, Luke 12:16-21)

4. Family disputes because we have accepted the faith (Luke 14:26; Matt. 10:34-39)

As delineated in the Sermon on the Mount (Matthew 6:25-34)—

5. Our meals
6. Our fashions
7. Our tomorrows

We must put the Lord Jesus Christ absolutely first in our lives and, as Peter suggested, cast all our anxiety on him, for he cares for us and is willing to bear all our burdens (1 Pet. 5:7). The Apostle Paul wrote to the Philippians, "Be anxious for nothing, but in everything, by prayer and supplication with thanksgiving, let your requests be made known unto God. And the peace of God, which passeth all understanding, shall keep your hearts and minds through Christ Jesus" (Phil. 4:6, 7, KJV). In the midst of a world of pressure and anxiety, the God of the universe gives peace and comfort.

As I have said, while anxiety in the form of fret and worry is wrong and should be yielded to Christ, anxiety in the form of realistic, legitimate concern is healthy. In the same letter to the Philippians, in which Paul said to "have no anxiety," he also spoke approvingly of Timothy being genuinely anxious for the welfare of the church at Philippi. Our Lord told us that we should be very anxious about one thing—our souls. He said, "What profit is there if you gain the whole world—and lose eternal life? What can be compared with the value of eternal life?" (Matt. 16:26). Our Lord does not mean that worldly activities are unnecessary. He only said that if we were fearful about our souls, our lesser fears would dissolve. He said, "... and he will give them to you if you give him first place in your life and live as he wants you to" (Matt. 6:33).

It used to be that the true Christian was set apart from others by the intensity of his healthy anxiety concerning his soul. Modern souls do not know it, but the things that they have been most anxious about are only worthless substitutes for Christ, who alone can calm their spirit. Charlatans advise to forget eternity and concentrate on satisfying bodily desires. But who would want to be a contented cow? And what *real* answers are provided? Augustine was right when he said that our hearts were made for God, and that they are restless until they rest in him. The remedy, then, for anxiety and fear is a confident, trusting faith in the Lord Jesus Christ. In him we can exultantly triumph!

In the depths of his soul our Lord, in Gethsemane, suffered anguish the like of which men have never known. The Word of God says, "... for he was in such agony of spirit that he broke into a sweat of blood, with great drops falling to the ground ..." (Luke 22:44). This is the symptom of extreme anguish of mind that is rarely witnessed. The courage of our Lord is not the negative quality based on literal fearlessness; the measure of his courage was the measure of his ability to overcome fear. One would have been impossible without the other, and when the shadow of the cross loomed up so close to him that he even cried, "If you are willing, please take away this cup

106

of horror from me ..." (Luke 22:42), he proceeded to take such an attitude towards calamity that he wrung from the situation the courage that made him our triumphant Redeemer and Savior. And because he was triumphant in that dark hour, mastering and conquering fear, so can we conquer also, by faith in him!

◆ ◆ ◆

*For God hath not given us
the spirit of fear, but of power, and of love, and of a
sound mind.*
2 TIMOTHY 1:7, KJV

*We need have no fear of someone
who loves us perfectly; his perfect love for us
eliminates all dread of what he might do to us. If we
are afraid, it is for fear of what he might do to us, and
shows that we are not fully convinced
that he really loves us.*
1 JOHN 4:18

CHAPTER SIX

You have to live with yourself

William Glasser, M.D., presents in his book *Reality Therapy* a new approach to psychiatry. In it he breaks with Freudian analysis in both theory and practice and challenges the validity of the six postulates listed as characterizing most forms of professional psychotherapy now practiced in the United States. O. Hobart Mowrer, Research Professor of Psychology of the University of Illinois, points out in the foreword these six postulates or presuppositions. 1. The reality of mental illness; 2. The reconstructive exploration of the patient's past; 3. Transference; 4. An "unconscious" which must be plumbed; 5. Interpretation rather than evaluation of behavior; and 6. Change through insight and permissiveness.

Dr. Glasser states that the conventional therapist attempts to remain as impersonal and objective as possible, never becoming involved as a person in the patient's life. In *reality therapy,* the therapist becomes both involved and very real to the patient. In essence, *reality therapy* depends upon what could be called a psychiatric version of the three R's: Reality, Responsibility, and Right-and-Wrong.

The problem with those who seek psychiatric treatment, Dr. Glasser suggests, is that their needs are not being satisfied. Here is immediately seen a great difference between *reality therapy* and *psychoanalysis:* To Freud, the needs which are presumably unfulfilled in the so-called neurotic person are those of sex and aggression; to Glasser the basic human needs are for relatedness and respect. And when it is asked how one satisfies these needs, the answer is found by doing what is realistic, responsible, and right. This is obviously New Testament psychology. But one element is missing: Where does the motivation, power, and ability come from to *do* what is realistic, responsible, and right?

Allan Fromme, in his book *Our Troubled Selves,* points out that the conventional psychologist does not view guilt or its cause in moral terms. Man's desires are neither good nor bad: they are simply there—an indelible part of man's being. Glasser, on the other hand, takes the New Testament approach and *does* view guilt in moral terms, asserting that there is no valid solution to guilt unless it is viewed in moral terms. But again, where does the motivation, power, and ability come from?

Dr. Smiley Blanton, the psychiatrist, said that there is a precept inherent in all religious teaching, that if an individual seeks to better his life, there is a definite way to do it. First, there must be a conviction of personal sin or wrongdoing. Second, there must be repentance or a desire to lead a better life. Third, restitution must be made to those who have been injured or wronged. Fourth, there must be some kind of a punitive experience, an atonement. (This, of course, gives tremendous significance to the vicarious death of our Lord Jesus Christ, who died "... once for the sins of all us guilty sinners, although he himself was innocent of any sin at any time, that he might bring us safely home to God" (1 Pet. 3:18). Restitution is tied so closely with forgiveness that when we realize our sins are paid for and forgiven, the natural response is to want to forgive others and make restitution an act of worship and thanksgiving. Men can never find an adequate forgiveness apart from the reconciliation with God that is promised through faith in Jesus Christ's great redemptive work at Calvary.) The final step is changed behavior. Like the woman taken in adultery, we must go our way and sin no more. We must yield ourselves to the living Christ and commit our lives to him. We are then able to "take up" life again.

It is virtually impossible for one to journey through life carrying the ever-mounting burden of a constantly disapproving conscience. This reminds me of Ernest Renan's statement that the twentieth century will spend a good deal of its time picking out of the wastebasket things that the nineteenth century threw into it. One of the things now being retrieved is this necessity for the mind to be absolved from guilt. We cannot live with guilt; that is, *truly live*. The pagan psychologist says, "Lower your standards; learn to do as you please without feeling guilty." This is Freud's early

110

solution, and one that has today been widely accepted in our culture. But because it deals only with *subjective guilt* feelings and not *objective guilt,* it rarely works. So, now our most modern psychologists are unknowingly bringing us right back to the plain teaching of the Word of God about how to find relief from guilt.

You must live with yourself, your projected *self-image.* Someone has said, "A man can stand a lot as long as he can stand himself." It is absolutely essential that every man cultivate at all costs a *self* with whom he can live in peace and happiness, in other words, a *self-image* that he can respect. He must look to his conscience with a desire to eradicate the sense of guilt.

Lord Byron, when fleeing from England, asked, "What exile from himself can flee?" A man may flee from other men, from familiar scenes and from the obligations of life, and he may even become a recluse in some obscure corner of the earth; he may repudiate the establishment and turn his back on his early training and beliefs, but from himself there is no escape.

A young man committed a grievous wrong and fled. He traveled all over the world, but could find no peace or satisfaction. Finally he confessed, "Everywhere I go I am still myself, and I myself am the penalty for the wrong." There was no way he could escape or repair his *self-image;* he was locked in. I am reminded of the words of Jesus to the people of Israel, "And now your house is left to you, desolate" (Matt. 23:38).

It is one of the inescapable facts of life that we

111

have to live with what we are. For some this is romance, for others it is intolerable boredom and depression. For still others it is radiant exuberance and joy; life is a thrilling, challenging adventure. What happiness and pleasure there is in living with a *projected image* that you can love and respect! And, conversely, there is no worse hell than to live with a *self* you hate and cannot respect. A young man was asked why he did not steal a large amount of money when there was once an opportunity, and at the same time there was no possibility that he would ever be caught. He replied thoughtfully, "Because I did not want to spend the rest of my life with a thief."

There are myriads of people who have divided and conflicting personalities. In them is a contentious spirit; they are at odds with themselves most of the time and are therefore disagreeable and are likely to be irritable in their relationships with others. They are like one of the characters in a novel about whom the author says, "He was not a personality; he was a civil war."

When a *self* is stung by remorse and haunted by a sense of guilt over wrongs committed, it becomes highly self-conscious, because it is concerned only with *self*. Such a *self* is what the Apostle Paul calls "the flesh," the "carnal mind," which is at enmity with both God and man (Rom. 8:7). Psychiatrists are now saying what ministers have always said—that a clear mind free of or forgiven for wrongdoing is essential to the harmonious organization of a man's personality. Marcus Aurelius, one of the world's wisest men, knew the

importance of this truth. He said that the one thing worth living for is to keep one's soul pure. Freedom from guilt, a healthy mind, and a glorious wholeness is Jesus Christ's contribution to men. Faith in him offers a cleansing catharsis that removes the sense of guilt and puts in its place the exuberant joy of acceptance, forgiveness, and a healthy mind.

What is a sense of guilt? Psychologists speak of two categories: *objective* and *subjective guilt.* The former exists apart from our feelings. Here the person has broken some legal standard and he is guilty, whether he feels it or not. The latter, *subjective guilt,* is a feeling or inner experience of remorse because of one's actions. The *objective guilt* upon which this feeling of *subjective guilt* is based may not be a valid reason for feeling guilty, but it has nothing to do with the emotion. From the biblical point of view, *objective guilt* is what the Word of God calls "sin," and *subjective guilt* is the *direct result of* sin.

Sin, or a resultant sense of guilt, has a peculiar damaging effect on our personalities. I believe the closest analogy would be that of a festering wound. Guilt cuts deeper and deeper into the emotional and spiritual nature. The one who sins may at first feel no pain; he may feel that he has "gotten away with it." But if, like the history of some physical diseases, the development is slow, the time nevertheless will come when this malady of guilt begins to cause trouble. All of a sudden it may "break out"—tension increases, nervousness becomes a problem, and curious obsessions de-

velop. One man, for instance, always had to go back to try a door after he locked it. Another constantly washed his hands after touching things. Perhaps, like Lady Macbeth, he was trying to wash out a spot which did not exist on his hands, but was indelibly printed in his mind.

Frequently the obsessions are much deeper and result in acute, unrelieved suffering. The mind becomes unsettled, the emotions are thrown out of gear, and one becomes desperately unhappy and increasingly ineffective. One explanation of this phenomenon is that guilt can be appropriately described as an unclean wound. In contrast, such healthy feelings as sorrow may be described as clean wounds. A clean wound in the flesh heals with little difficulty, according to the processes of nature. A tree hit by lightning gradually heals over its wounds. But the effect of unrelieved guilt or sin is quite another matter. Being unclean, the normal healing processes are inoperative, ineffective. The infection of guilt increases and spreads through the body, the mind, and the spirit. The more that guilt is rationalized away and protected from open recognition, the more acute it becomes. Nature always strives to isolate an infection center, but in the case of guilt it cannot be done. In youth and even in the strong middle years its injurious effects may in part be halted. But with the declining vitality of advancing years and the heavier burden of responsibility which comes with maturity, resistance gradually declines, and frequently the long hidden infection of guilt at last becomes a malignancy that dominates the en-

tire system. We often hear of men breaking down, having heart trouble, high blood pressure, abnormal tensions, or a vague, unaccountable dissatisfaction that tends to spoil their happiness. Not always, of course, is a sense of guilt at the root of such difficulty, but frequently it is. In personal counseling it has been discovered that a great number of those who were examined in such a condition were also suffering from an unrelieved burden of *subjective guilt*.

We are living in a generation that has tried hard to accept the *amoral* approach of men such as Allan Fromme, who do not view guilt in moral terms, and who deny the reality of sin altogether. One of the profound causes of the nervous tensions of this era is that it does not recognize and properly deal with today's magnitude of guilt and its malignancy in human minds. It may also be that the enormous social sins of our times are sapping the mental and emotional health of modern man. People seem to have the idea that they can sin with impunity, but the strange part of it is that sin gets into their system, and soon begins to discharge what amounts to a "poison"—unhealthy, deteriorating secretions that flow from an unrelieved sense of guilt. When this poison gets into your thinking you say to yourself, "I don't seem to be happy. I don't enjoy anything anymore. I'm distraught, irritable, upset. Everything has a bad taste. I'm tired all the time. What is the matter with everybody; what is the matter with me?" How this vindicates the truth of the Word of God: "... you may be sure that your sin will catch up with you" (Num. 32:23); "Don't be misled; remember that you can't ignore God and get away with it: a man will always reap just the kind of crop he sows!" (Gal. 6:7).

Prominent physicians have proven the theory that hate and resentment can cause definite physical ailments. There are many laboratory records available in support of these facts. You simply cannot allow the poison of guilt to remain in your mind and at the same time be happy and efficient. There are those who pathetically attempt to rationalize sin. In so doing they berate themselves and develop a *projected image* they could never respect, but that can only make them miserable and unhappy. In this respect, how glorious are the words of the apostle in 2 Corinthians 5:17: "When someone becomes a Christian he becomes a brand new person inside. He is not the same any more. A new life has begun!" Christ has the power to change the worst kind of a *self* into a *glorious self*. This is what conversion really means—a cleansing change from an old life of misery to the new life in Christ!

A sense of guilt also originates from the failure to live up to our own standards and value systems. When we violate our convictions, whatever they might be, we immediately feel a sense of estrangement or separation; we become fragmented and disharmonized.

First of all, there is the estrangement of *self*. Dr. John MacKay says that one aspect of a sinner is that he is a human being who has become a problem to himself. If you live with a *self-image* you cannot respect, you are on the road to self-loathing. You will become so weary of the claiming presence of guilt that you will cry out as did the wild man of Gadara to be let alone! There is a striking passage in the book of Revelation that says, "It was sweet in my mouth but it gave me a stomach ache when I swallowed it" (Rev. 10:10).

Dr. E. Stanley Jones reminds us of the story of the woman in Nathaniel Hawthorne's *The Scarlet Letter* who, as punishment, was compelled to wear a huge scarlet letter "A" for Adulteress. It flared before everyone to her shame. But the man with whom she committed the act was scot-free, because no one knew who he was. No one knew? *He* knew, and now and again he was seen clutching at his heart as if in pain. Then, one fateful day he fell in a swoon before the assembled hosts, and in falling tore open his shirt. When men stooped to pick him up they found written over his heart the scarlet letter "A"—written in his own blood. He had not escaped. No one does, for "Thou shalt not commit adultery" is written not merely in the tables of stone, but in the very constitution of our being. Every adulterer wears the scarlet letter of guilt over his heart. The sparkle of purity is gone, and dullness, the sign of inward death, gives away the case to both the man and to the world. He may profess his innocence with vehemence of swearing as did Peter at the denial of his Master, but still the cock crows. Nature betrays him, and his false world of self-justification falls to pieces. He stumbles out and "weeps bitterly" because he has not lived up to his own standards.

Every jet passenger plane carries an instrument, locked and sealed in an almost indestructible box, which records everything that transpires on each flight. At the end of a journey the instrument is unsealed, and no matter what the pilot may say, the record is there. In the event of an accident, it can provide an evaluation of the cause. It is a mechanical conscience, but one no more accurate than the conscience sealed within us at the very depths of our being. Its key is not in our hand; it is in the hands of our Maker, and the record is absolutely correct—down to the recording of thought, intention, and emotion. And there is no appeal from it.

The moving finger writes,
And having writ, moves on;
Nor all your Piety nor Wit
Shall lure it back to cancel half a Line,
Nor all your Tears wash out a Word of it.

Edward Fitzgerald

Everything is recorded and stored in our minds as though our brain was a computer. Some amazing discoveries have been made with respect to the brain. Once recorded, nothing is ever forgotten; there is only the inability to recall. When given the proper stimulus, not only can the mind replay the event, but it can also immediately duplicate the emotions that accompanied that event.

The Holy Book teaches us that every unrepentant, unregenerate man will face the record of his deeds at the Judgment Bar of a holy God. But what men do not realize is that there is a *judgment bar* in life. Theologians have been saying for centuries that men are profoundly affected by their sins. Now we're hearing it from men of science. Their voice is quite low and deliberate; they do not shout it, but it is terrifying. Dr. Stanley Cobb says that out of hundreds of cases of sufferers from arthritis, asthma, and mucous colitis, 68 percent expressed feelings of guilt. A sense of guilt had worked itself into the physical life, bringing havoc and disease in the form of three diseases, although we can be quite sure it works out in a multitude of others. In the procedure of the lie detector test, when a man tells a lie, his blood pressure goes up; when he tells the truth, it stays normal.

A prominent judge in the court of domestic relations became severely ill with a nervous disorder. When every avenue of diagnosis failed, he finally confessed to his physician that he had been keeping a mistress. This conflict within him brought on his trouble and destroyed his effectiveness and peace.

No wonder that Dr. Link, after years of dealing with maladjusted people, was forced to realize that the findings of psychology, in respect to personality, were largely a rediscovery of old religious truths. Isaiah recognized the connection between forgiveness and healing of sickness. He said, "The people of Israel will no longer say, 'We are sick and helpless,' for the Lord will forgive them their sins and bless them" (Isa. 33:24).

Many non-Christian psychologists today advise their patients who have hates to continue their hates, lest by suppression a complex be set up, or for those who have trouble with sex to go to a prostitute, from the same fear of the formation of a complex. In two such cases where the advice was followed, the results were disastrous. In one, continued hate wore the person out physically and left her exhausted, and in the other, promiscuity produced a sense of guilt and physical health grew worse. But in both cases, when they faced the wrong, confessed it and found forgiveness in the grace of God as proffered in the wounds of Jesus Christ, there was release and a total healing.

Second, a sense of guilt leads to a separation of man from man. There is no cement in sin; it is centrifugal and dividing. The essence of sin is self-will, and this self-will is bound to run against self-will in others. Hence, by its very nature, sin is bound to be disruptive in human relationships.

An extremely ill man went to a physician, and the doctor began to probe for causes. After much resistance the man admitted that when his father died and left an estate he was made the executor of the will, and he purposely kept back part of his brother's share. He stole it. The physician insisted that he make restitution and write to his brother and confess it. When the letter was dropped in the mail box he said, "Thank God, the burden is gone." He was a well man from that hour.

Third, a sense of guilt separates men from God. This is the supreme alienation. The Scripture declares "... your sins have cut you off from God..." (Isa. 59:2). This is precisely where the mediation of our Lord Jesus Christ means the most to us. We are all conscious of the fact that we have come

120

short of the glory of God. We have failed; we have missed the mark. But Jesus Christ opens to us the way whereby sinful man can find his way back in complete forgiveness, and reconciliation to a holy God. This estrangement from God is the most serious of all, for unless we are assured that we are reconciled to the Great Center of things, we are all out of gear. No matter how we may try to forget this or gloss over it, there is a great emptiness and meaninglessness that will not let up when we know we are alienated from God. When we attempt to rationalize sin, our desires draw arguments to themselves like a magnet draws iron filings. We seldom *think* with only our minds, our pure intellect; we *think* primarily with our emotions. Forgiveness, relief, and reconciliation come only when we are absolutely honest, frank, and thorough in admitting the existence of sin in our lives, the desire to be delivered from it, and the need for forgiveness.

Jesus said to the man who was sick of a palsy, "... Cheer up, for I have forgiven your sins!" (Matt. 9:2). Evidently, in this man's case, the sickness of his body was rooted in the central sickness and alienation of his soul, and he could never be well until forgiveness cleansed away the inner poison of guilt. This, of course, does not mean that all sickness is caused by guilt—that would be absurd. But our Lord knew what men are just now scientifically discovering—that there is indeed a very real connection between sin and disease. How glorious that our Lord has the answer to the problem of sin in human life! What quinine is to malaria, insulin is to diabetes, and Salk vaccine is to poliomyelitis, the cross is to guilt.

There is a remedy for guilt. First, we must recognize as David did that in committing wrongs we are actually sinning against God, who alone is sinless. Sin is a violation of the moral order of God. David wrote, "O loving and kind God, have mercy. Have pity upon me and take away the awful stain of my transgressions. Oh, wash me, cleanse me from this guilt. Let me be pure again. For I admit my shameful deed—it haunts me day and night. It is against you and you alone I sinned, and did this terrible thing. You saw it all, and your sentence against me is just" (Ps. 51:1-4). We must recognize that apart from God no man can really do good and that our own so-called righteous acts are really as acceptable to God as a pile of filthy rags (Isa. 64:6). In short, we must be sincerely ashamed and sorry that we have sinned against a holy God.

Second, we must put everything right that can be put right. And we should start by breaking with the thing that is destroying us. Said Zacchaeus in that triumphant hour of repentance when he entered the new world Christ offers to all of us, "... If I find I have overcharged anyone on his taxes, I will penalize myself by giving him back four times as much!" (Luke 19:8). Even before we come to God and ask for his forgiveness, our earnest penitence ought to be carried out. We must be reconciled to our brother before we come to the altar (Matt. 5:23, 24).

Third, we must realize forgiveness of God.

122

There is a wideness in God's mercy. No matter how enormous our sin, we have a perfect forgiveness and expiation in the atonement provided in the sacrificial death of Jesus Christ. This is grace—*to be accepted in the Beloved.*

We must never forget that the pride of self-righteousness is as hellish and evil as the fleshly sin of harlot and the libertine. If anything, it is worse. Our Lord loves sinners, but he hates the sin, and he loathes self-righteousness. We read in 2 Corinthians 5:21: "For God took the sinless Christ and poured into him our sins. Then, in exchange, he poured God's goodness into us!" We have the glorious promise of 1 John 1:9: "But if we confess our sins to him, he can be depended on to forgive us and to cleanse us from every wrong."

But it is not enough to know with the *mind* that we are forgiven. We must accept the forgiveness that is offered and allow this glorious truth to penetrate our heart—*we are forgiven!* Some people find they have to say it over and over to themselves until it dawns on them like the glory of a clear, beautiful summer morning that they are actually, truly forgiven from the bondage of sin's guilt!

To be forgiven means that a relationship is restored. To be forgiven means that the relationship between you and God is as though you had *never sinned.* The Prodigal Son may have had to be nursed in body and mind after his venture into the far country, but he was a son, not a swineherd, and the effect of that on the spirit is a tonic the value of which cannot be exaggerated.

Forgiveness also means a new beginning. The prison doors are open, and blue skies and sunshine and the great open spaces are before you. The words of God regarding forgiveness have tremendous significance: Our sins are "blotted out," "put behind God's back," "to be remembered no more forever," "as far as the east is from the west," "as high as heaven is from the earth, they are removed from us." The antitoxin of Christ's blood has defeated the disease of sin forever! And so it is not trite to say that *today is the first day of the rest of your life.* Make it a new day, a glorious and beautiful day!

These things being so, there is a sense in which we must forgive ourselves our own sins; we too must put them behind our backs. If God has put them behind his back we are not to be poking around his back dragging our sins out and wearing them around our necks again. We must realize that we have been forgiven of God, our relationship is restored, and we are starting again as new persons. Do not allow the memory of past sins to haunt your mind like an evil specter. God's promise is valid: "... No matter how deep the stain of your sins, I can take it out and make you as clean as freshly fallen snow" (Isa. 1:18). Grace has changed your *state*.

Prayer can do much in preventing the memory of past sins from destroying your effectiveness. The great apostle knew the ghastly nightmare of sin's remorse, but once forgiven he said, "... Forgetting the past and looking forward to what lies ahead, I strain to reach the end of the race and receive the prize for which God is calling us up to heaven because of what Christ Jesus did for us" (Phil. 3:13, 14). Forget and press on— happiness is ahead! The glory of the Person of Christ and the atonement he wrought on the cross of Calvary brings to distressed minds the knowledge of God's forgiveness, ushering in that wonderful peace that passes all understanding.

◆ ◆ ◆

But if you don't do as you have said, then you will have sinned against the Lord, and you may be sure that your sin will catch up with you.
NUMBERS 32:23

A man who refuses to admit his mistakes can never be successful. But if he confesses and forsakes them, he gets another chance.
PROVERBS 28:13

CHAPTER SEVEN

Peace in a troubled world

A London newspaper once carried an interesting story of a man whose sight had been recently restored. Having been blind from the age of two, he did not remember how the world and his fellow men had appeared. One of the most striking notions he had formed in his sightlessness, however, was that all human faces looked peaceful. We must believe that human faces were meant by God to look peaceful, but indeed it is the rare exception, not the rule. We live in a time of intensified stress and strain. Dr. Ernest R. Hilgard, former president of the American Psychology Association and a distinguished psychologist, points out that the causes of contemporary anxiety are complex; included in these are the two world wars within our century and a cold war persisting since the last one, the increasing mobility of peoples—geographically and economically—disturbing the sense of rootedness, and shifting values so that parents are overwhelmed with philosophies about child rearing practices, moral standards, and religious beliefs. All of these factors, plus a multitude of personal problems, are manifesting themselves today physically.

This is an era of heart disease, high blood pressure, and nervous breakdowns. These afflictions frequently have their origin in largely hectic and frantic minds rather than in physical causes. William Muldoon, the famous athletic trainer, once said that people do not die of disease, but of internal combustion. Hypertension is a prevailing American malady. Dr. Alvarez, formerly of the Mayo Clinic, says that we little realize the number of human diseases that are either begun or accentuated by worry. For multitudes of nervous, intense, high-strung people, life is a constant, unrelieved strain.

M. A. Mortenson, M.D., of the Battle Creek Sanitarium, says that American business and professional men are not living out their normal life expectancies. Worry, uncertainty, and the tensions and pressures of these troubled times, together with the pace of American life, are wreaking havoc among men of forty or more years of age; many are dying altogether too soon. Heart disease, high blood pressure, arterial disease, kidney disease, nervous disorders, cancers, gastrointestinal troubles—these are the worst enemies of America's men of responsibility and leadership. Note that few of these are germ-caused diseases. They fall into the classification of degenerative diseases.

Modern medicine can now control many of the viral and germ-caused diseases that have taken such enormous tolls in the past, including typhoid, scarlet fever, diphtheria, small pox, and poliomyelitis; but the troubles that are today mowing down many of our most valuable people of forty or more years of age are the degenerative diseases which come about because of the age of the individual plus wrong living habits, overwork, stress, strain, excesses in sex, nicotine, alcohol, wrong diet, overweight, too little rest and relaxation, and heightened blood pressure. It is estimated that 25 percent of all deaths of men over fifty are due to hypertension. A physician from John Hopkins Hospital said that we do not know why worriers die sooner than nonworriers, but we do know that it is a fact.

Evidently we were inwardly constructed by God for faith, not fear and worry. Therefore, the need of faith is not something imposed on us dogmatically; it is written into us intrinsically. The late E. Stanley Jones said that the kingdom of God is in our bloodstream. To live by worry is to live against reality. Worry and anxiety keep us from being our best; they paralyze the center of life. He tells of an incident of a Mexican gentleman who saw a snake and was pricked by a barbed wire at the same moment. Thinking he was bitten by the snake, he foamed at the mouth and acted as though he were about to die. When a doctor arrived and saw there was no swelling at the abrasion, he assured him that he had not been bitten. The man got well almost instantly.

Interestingly, the word "worry" is derived from an Anglo-Saxon word meaning "to choke." Dr. Seward Wood, head of the Medical School at the University of Oklahoma, gave an address before the nose and throat section of the American Medical Association on the relation of worry to the common cold, the infection of the sinuses, and asthma. He told of a young woman who could turn asthma on and off by turning worry on and off, and of a salesman who invariably developed inflammation of the membranes of the nose when his mother-in-law was due to arrive for a visit.

It has been said that the chronic worrier develops a small chest because he is afraid to breathe deeply; he is afraid of the healing of fresh air, of God's hope, and God's power. The one who worries is actually saying, "I cannot trust God. I'll take things into my own hands." And the inevitable result is frustration and the incapacity to meet the dreaded thing when it does come. But the one who is absolutely committed to Jesus Christ can meet it, overcome it, and assimilate it into the purpose of his life.

Without doubt, the greatest legacy our matchless Christ left this world was his peace. Someone has said that he had nothing else to leave. He was the poorest of the poor; he had no material possessions of any kind to divide among the men he loved, and so he bequeathed to them the one thing that was in his power to give—his peace—the *peace* that was his in those terrible hours when the crucificial hammers were plied against his hands and feet. He said, "I am leaving you with a gift—peace of mind and heart! And the peace I give isn't fragile like the peace the world gives. So don't be troubled or afraid" (John 14:27).

A great saint of God who had given his life to

the Christian ministry, whose very countenance was ablaze with the light of Christ, said to a young minister, "My son, I do not pray that you shall have what the world calls success. I do not pray that you shall acquire possessions, but I do pray that you shall have peace in your mind and heart." And then with tenderness he gave the ancient benediction: "The Lord bless thee, and keep thee; the Lord make his face to shine upon thee, and be gracious unto thee; the Lord lift up his countenance upon thee, and give thee peace."

Apart from a vital, living relationship with Jesus Christ, this peace is not known. It is not easy to achieve inner peace today or to maintain it unbroken against the assaults and the invasions of this untranquil, disturbed, and disturbing world. That more people now than ever before are high-strung, nervously irritable, and lacking in repose, is not surprising. The general insecurity of the present time registers itself not only politically and economically, but the toll it takes emotionally and mentally is even more serious. Enigmatically, people are frantic in their search for peace!

True indeed, we are living in trying times, and we can blame much of the responsibility for nervous breakdowns and frustrated lives on the circumstances—but not all. The trouble lies deeper, for when we look into our own hearts and explore the causes of our own restless moods and feelings, we have to admit that it is our own fault. The trouble lies within, and when we are completely honest with ourselves we realize that it is because we lack one thing—the appropriation of the legacy of peace Jesus left us.

I am confident that there has never been a person anywhere or anytime who has not desired peace in his heart—not necessarily the peace of reconciliation *with* God, but the peace *of* God. And I do not mean the peace of lethargic ease or of a self-protected, sheltered life; nor do I mean the peace of an emotional stoic who achieves calm by doing violence to his affections and by dampening down the fires of love, involvement, compassion and pity in his heart. I mean the peace that stands as a sentinel at the gateway of the soul and confronts all manner of difficulties with courageous, steady eyes, the peace that holds the heart serene through hectic days and blasts of unjust criticisms from men. Our matchless Lord promises to the one whose life is hid in him a sufficient refuge for the soul—his peace! Our Lord did not often speak about it, but on every page of the Gospels you can feel its overwhelming intensity!

Consider the sublimity of the serenity of our Lord Jesus Christ. Did anyone while watching our Lord in those Galilean days ever see him irritated? Think of what he had to put up with, and how in the midst of it all he remained serene. There were the continual intrusions upon his privacy, with no respite from dawn to dark, the steady drain on his spiritual resources, the breaking in on his hours of quiet by inconsiderate people, the awful burden of sharing every aching heart, sin, and sorrow, and of feeling these personally as if they were his own. There were the misunderstandings, the sharp, cutting criticisms, the pettiness of people, the venomous, vitriolic hatred of the Pharisees, the disdain and scorn of the Sadducees, the terrible, unremitting toil, the disappointment, the crushing load of such a life, and at last the broken heart—broken through the agony of unrequited love; and yet, through it all, the same serene, untroubled countenance. There was no flurry, no sign of strain, no evidence of nerves giving way; always "my peace." Certainly the world has never seen anything more marvelous than the poise and tranquility of our Lord Jesus Christ.

Contrast his disciples. Their nerves often gave way. When they were about to leave a Samaritan village that was rude and inhospitable, they said with anger, "Lord, let us call down fire from heaven—let's teach these ungrateful people a lesson" (Luke 9:54†)! Jesus turned to them and said, "Ye know not what manner of spirit ye are of..." (vs. 55, KJV). Always that calm center, that unabating serenity.

One night on the Sea of Gennesaret, when the disciples' frail boat was being tossed about by tempestuous waves, they shouted, as all self-control was flung to the four winds, "Teacher, don't you even care that we are all about to drown?" (Mark 4:38). But our Lord answered, "Peace, be still" (vs. 39, KJV). He was speaking just as much to the disciples as he was to the waves that obeyed him. Always that inner calm—"Peace, be still."

A crowd of five thousand followed them one day to their secret retreat in the wilderness. The disciples, weary of the crowd, the pressure, and confusion, said, "Send the crowds away..." (Matt. 14:15). But our Lord said, "They are sheep without a shepherd, and I love them" (Mark 6:34†). Always was that heart at leisure from itself.

Then came the end, when it seemed that everything went terribly wrong. The disciples knew something about the conspiracy against Christ in Jerusalem, so they implored him not to go there. But the Word of God says, "...He moved steadily onward towards Jerusalem with an iron will" (Luke 9:51). And when the enemy struck, their strained nerves snapped completely. The Scripture says, "At that point, all the disciples deserted him and fled" (Matt. 26:56).

But consider our Lord before the Sanhedrin, on the road to Skull Hill, in the midst of a raucous mob that mocked him in his death agony, when he prayed on behalf of his murderers, "Father, forgive these people, for they don't know what they are doing" (Luke 23:34). Consider his last words—"Father, I commit my spirit to you" (Luke 23:46). Indeed, *there* was a composure the like of which man can never know apart from Jesus Christ. All the way from Bethlehem to Nazareth to Calvary there was evidence of his virile, powerful peace!

But you say, "But that was Jesus; he was different. We are only common clay. You cannot expect us to achieve that poise of soul, that spirit of serenity. It was magnificent, but for us it is utterly and forever impossible!" Oh, but if I could convince one troubled heart that this wonderful gift,

133

"the peace of Christ," which is the peace of God that passes all understanding, is *not* a far-off dream, but is within the reach of *anyone* who will claim it! The real marvel is not only to hear throughout the story of our Lord, from the carpenter's bench to the cross, the deep, central theme—"My peace," but to hear him saying, "My peace I *give* unto you. To you who know what it means to be rushed, fretful, agitated, and worried—my peace to *you!*"

What is this peace Christ offers to us?

1. It is the peace of *adequate resources*. There can be few things more wearing to the nerves than to face life or some difficult task in life with insufficient spiritual resources. C. E. Montague said that this is the real curse of Adam—not the work itself, but the worry and the doubt of ever getting it done! The consciousness of inadequate resources can drive a man to utter distraction. It can cause sleepless nights, unrelieved strain, impairment of the mind, and deteriorating health; it can weigh down upon a man until he is totally miserable.

But there was nothing of that in our Lord Jesus Christ. He moved from one task to another evidently without halting or haste. I believe he never had the haggard look of one who has reached his limit. Yet he spent himself without stint; he was expendable. But no matter how much he gave, his resources were never exhausted. He was free from all the effects of worry and trouble that lay waste so many lesser souls.

2. The peace of Christ is the peace of *supreme adequacy for life*. This he offers to us for the

crowded days when the pressure of work becomes a nightmare, for the fearsome responsibilities that we often would like to flee, for the terrible exigencies of crisis and tragedy that take us completely unaware. He can make us feel equal to this difficult, puzzling maze we call life, and he can give us, if we will open our hearts to him, the indwelling presence of the blessed Person of the Holy Spirit. This is the supreme resource. To possess it is to possess an enduring peace and adequacy sufficient for anything life may bring.

Fasten your attention on Christ, for it is the law of the mind that whatever gets your attention gets *you*. That is why the apostle said, "Let heaven fill your thoughts; don't spend your time worrying about things down here" (Col. 3:2). The writer of Hebrews admonishes us to lay aside earthly cares and "Keep your eyes on Jesus, our leader and instructor..." (Heb. 12:2). If your worries get your attention, they'll get you; if Christ gets your attention, he'll get you. Fear and worry tighten you up, but faith relaxes. It has been said that worry keeps the motor running even after you're parked. God said through the prophet Isaiah, "...In quietness and confidence is your strength..." (Isa. 30:15). You must quiet everything in the quietness of God. Still your being before him and drink in his strength. Let his presence and power permeate every pore of your being and bathe the tired and restless nerve cells with his healing.

General Jackson could say that he felt as safe on the battlefield as in bed, because his trust was in God. But with that quietness there must be confidence in God through commitment to Jesus Christ, because in having him we have *everything*. The Word of God says, "...Don't worry about *things*—food, drink, and clothes. For you already have life and a body—and they are far more important than what to eat and wear" (Matt. 6:25). "But seek ye first the kingdom of God, and his righteousness, and all these things shall be added unto you" (Matt. 6:33, KJV). This means exactly what it says! We are not to worry about even the basic necessities of life. Instead we are to strive for inner peace, mental, emotional, and spiritual harmony, developing an organized, integrated, and radiant personality. And because the life of Christ is being lived through us, in our total surrender to the Spirit of God, we will be able to meet life effectively and triumphantly, no matter what the circumstances! With this kind of dependence on the adequate resources of Jesus Christ, the necessary things of life *will* be added unto us. Habitual resting of our worries upon the goodness of God through faith releases power into our lives that otherwise would not be possible. Our only legitimate "worries" are our relationship to Jesus Christ, our spiritual growth, and our love and concern for others.

3. The peace of our Lord Jesus Christ is the peace of a *disciplined life*. Sooner or later we all discover that slackness of any kind, whether in work, thought, or life, is always destructive of inner repose. Restlessness and unhappiness are the inevitable nemesis of the life of passing whim and purposeless drift. Whenever you see reflected

136

in the face of some man or woman the radiance of a deep inner serenity, you may safely say, "There has been discipline there," the discipline of time, thought, and desire.

Dr. Link has written that no life becomes all that it ought to be, in the well-roundedness of a well-integrated personality, unless it is thoroughly disciplined. We must discipline ourselves to meet today *today*. Our Lord showed very penetrating insight when he said, in Matthew 6:34, "So don't be anxious about tomorrow. God will take care of your tomorrow too. Live one day at a time," that is, today's own trouble is quite enough for today. He was not saying that there are no troubles to meet, for there are. Life is bound to bring troubles, but the disciplined life does not telescope the troubles of tomorrow and the next day into today. As one has rightly stated, "Live your life in day-tight compartments." If you put the troubles of next week into today by anticipating them through worry, you spoil today. You are meeting two sets of troubles—one set that is actually here, and the set that results from worrying about tomorrow's troubles. You are therefore meeting your troubles twice—once before they come and once when they are actually here. Such a telescoping of trouble is a double expenditure of needless energy.

Worry is the advance interest you pay on troubles that perhaps may never come. When they *do* come, you can meet and conquer each one separately. Dr. Leslie Weatherhead observed that the only plan he has ever found valuable in combating worry is to set out in the center of your mind the

137

situation about which you are worrying, and then write the situation out. If it is a decision that has to be made, thoughtfully list the pros and cons, then reckon up the situation as far as you can see it at that moment and say to yourself, "If that happens I will do this, or if this happens I will do that." If it is possible to take some positive action at once to resolve the worrying situation, then, of course, it should be done. It is very foolish to worry all night about some situation that you can remedy today, such as the simple writing of a letter.

Get your life organized, and set your priorities in proper order—with the hard and pressing tasks first. Don't let tasks pile up; do today what must be done today. And don't ever let emotion take the place of action. If you determine that something must be done, then do it! It is amazingly true that if we put our trust in the wisdom of God and in his power to help and guide us, we will never be completely mystified as to what is the right road to take. He always shows us where he would have us go when we trust and depend on him to lead us. In fact, if we are absolutely committed to him and are living in the center of his will, then whatever we want to do will be right. If we are in a right relationship with God, then anything we do is his will, because he said, "Be delighted with the Lord. Then he will give you all your heart's desires" (Ps. 37:4). "In everything you do, put God first, and he will direct you and crown your efforts with success" (Prov. 3:6). I don't believe that any *one thing* or any course of action exclusive of all others is necessarily the will of God. If I am in God's will, there are multitudes of things I could do that are in accordance with his purpose for my life. If I am in a right relationship with him, that which I want to do *most* is right and is what God wants me to do.

4. The peace of our Lord Jesus Christ is the peace of a *clean heart*. It does not matter how difficult life may be as long as the conscience is at rest. The real wreckers of the peace of the soul are not the slings and arrows of disappointed hopes, but the memories that sting because of sins still unconfessed, the divided loyalties that strike an uneasy bargain between the vision of God and the lure of the world, the breakdown of good-will and love, the resentments that brood in secret, the jealousies that torture the mind, and the temptations that are never seriously resisted.

There is only one cure for the infectious disease of sin and guilt, and that is to come to Christ in honest confession of your sin, to hear from him the blessed benediction of forgiveness, and then to rise in the glory of the peace that dwells only in the heart that is clean before God. David said, "Create in me a new clean heart, O God..." (Ps. 51:10). It is my conviction that the problem of sin in human life was solved in the death of our Lord Jesus Christ. If we have truly experienced the miracle of spiritual birth, our sins will not cause us to lose our salvation, but they will rob us of our joy, peace, and usefulness, and make us more miserable than unregenerate men. Indeed, if a believer continues to live in a way he knows is inconsistent with what *ought* to be, God may take that believer out of the world, because he is a source of embarrassment. Sin in the life of a believer will not cause that believer to be lost, but it can shorten his earthly life. The Scripture speaks of a sin "unto death" (James 5:19, 20; 1 John 5:16, 17; 1 Cor. 11:30 KJV).

5. The peace of Christ is the peace of *unbroken communion with God*. This is the great secret. When our Lord stole away from the clamorous crowds as the night descended, he was going to some lonely garden to rest his weary soul in fellowship with the Father. When he slipped out of the house at Bethany long before dawn was in the sky, while the village was still asleep, he was on his way to a lonely retreat where he would be in communion with the Father. When he entered the city streets where multitudes of hurt and ailing creatures waited hopefully for his coming, he was no longer weary as on the night before, but ready to meet that full day in the greatness of his strength, mighty to save. And the reason was that he had been on the mountaintop alone with the Father.

Man was structurally made for fellowship with God. When men do not live in fellowship with God, their lives sag, lose direction and meaning, and become increasingly empty. Dr. Carl Jung, though not inclined in a religious direction, summed up a patient's problems by saying that he was suffering from a loss of faith in God and in the future life.

The patient replied, "But Dr. Jung, do you believe these doctrines are true?"

Dr. Jung answered that it was no business of his,

140

that he was a physician, not a priest, and he could tell him only that if he recovered his faith he would get well—and if he didn't, he wouldn't get well.

Stop thinking you must carry your burden alone, and take to heart the words of 1 Peter 5:7: "Let him have all your worries and cares, for he is always thinking about you and watching everything that concerns you." It is never a waste of time at morning, midday, or at night, to thrust aside your pressing cares for five minutes, ten minutes, or an hour, and be still and remember God. The time thus diverted from ordinary tasks will more than be repaid by the poise and steadiness you will carry back to life from that secret place of the Most High. To have daily fellowship with God through our Lord Jesus Christ is to have found the peace that nothing in life can ever take away.

Edward Markham said that in the heart of a cyclone tearing the skies is a place of central calm. No matter how terrifying the storm, if you go down deep enough you will find the place of absolute stillness. The cyclone derives its power and driving energy from a calm center, coincidentally, the place of lowest pressure, and so does a man. That center in your life and mine should be the glorious Person of Jesus Christ.

Perhaps you have seen the toys that are so constructed that you cannot knock them down. No matter what position you put them in, they bounce right back into an upright position. An ocean liner is built on this same principle. Its base is curved and is filled below its bottom decks with tanks

141

containing thousands of gallons of fuel oil and water. This, plus the skill invested in the rest of its construction, gives it a flexibility so that no matter how it rides with the sea, it always rights itself.

If we fill our lives with the peace of Christ, we can take aboard the ship of our lives a base that will not only keep us afloat in times of storm, but will enable us to ride victoriously through every tempest of worry, fear or tragedy with great peace and spiritual flexibility.

◆ ◆ ◆

He will keep in perfect peace
all those who trust in him, whose thoughts
turn often to the Lord!
ISAIAH 26:3

"I have told you all this
so that you will have peace of heart and mind. Here on
earth you will have many trials and sorrows: but cheer
up, for I have overcome the world."
JOHN 16:33

CHAPTER EIGHT

Hidden possibilities

Many people today regard Christianity as ephemeral and theoretical because they view it entirely as theology or philosophy. Granted, Christianity fulfills itself adequately in both these fields, but it may also be thought of as a science. In fact, it is an exact science, for it is based on law. Higher than the science of psychology, it is the science of knowing God and of personal and social living. Learn its laws and you will invariably get equivalent and predictable results.

It is rather crude to think that the only laws existing in our universe are those that govern physical, material things. We are constantly finding, for example, new applications of power in the universe, and each one is regulated by law, as are all. One of the most recently discovered sources, of course, is atomic power. The average man scarcely knew this form of power existed, yet it has released such force that the world is startled.

Years ago the famous scientist Charles Steinmetz said that the greatest scientists of the future would be those who would chart and explain spiritual laws, such as those delineated in the New

Testament. This book has always been regarded as distinctly religious, but it may also be thought of as a formula book of *spiritual* science. That others have decried this possibility is no reason evangelicals should shy away from it. The New Testament contains procedures by which anyone who intelligently applies them can develop power in his mind and personality and become an instrument of God, in fulfillment of the promise of Acts 5:32: "The Holy Spirit ... is given by God to all who obey him." And it is the Holy Spirit who applies spiritual truth to our lives and, moreover, empowers us to live out that truth. The New Testament reveals hidden resources available to us, the nature of which most of us have never dreamed— spiritual forces equally as great, or perhaps greater and more valuable than all the laws that govern the material and physical world. A man who exercises confident, intelligent faith in the God of revelation can actually generate through prayer more energy than all the dynamos of the world.

One of the most glorious, but frequently neglected truths taught in the Word of God is that *God believes in us*. At the climax of his thrilling message through the prophet Isaiah, he declared, "For the mountains may depart and the hills disappear, but my kindness shall not leave you. My promise of peace for you will never be broken, says the Lord who has mercy upon you" (Isa. 54:10). It has been said that this promise was old when the world was young and will be young when the world has reached its final sunset. It is a promise that descends to the deepest depths of human

144

need and, bearing in its arms the priceless treasure of a rescued life, mounts up to the sublime heights of permanent safety and peace.

The mountains are the landmarks of the ages; the hills are the landscape of the continents. Together they stand for the order, symmetry, and beauty in the world. Order may yield to chaos and beauty may return to dust, but God's love for man abides, and his covenant of peace is eternal.

Let the picture of man in his sinfulness be painted as bleak and dark as the exigencies of dogma demand and history irrefutably proves. Man is a fallen creature, but he was made in the image of God. Though that image is marred, it is nevertheless there, and in the sight of God, man has infinite dignity and worth. Depraved though he may be, he is redeemable.

One of the tragedies of our century is that many outstanding philosophers, psychologists, and men of science have lost faith in man. Some predict despairingly that man has no future, that he is nothing but the accidental result of the impersonal, plus time, plus chance. According to molecular biologist Jacques Monod, man originated in a pre-biotic soup, and he has no future. Aldous Huxley concluded that there is no hope for man, that he is too weak ever to overcome his genetic stupidity. Men such as B. F. Skinner and Francis Crick view man as merely something that must be controlled. Others submit to the possibility of an elite leadership controlling man through genetic manipulation. Dr. Bentley Glass tells us that by the year 2000 a baby will be decanted from an artificial womb. With the cracking of the DNA code, we are promised that within a short time after that year we will have the ability to reproduce in endless numbers exact "carbon copy" human beings through the process called *cloning*. This will offer frightening possibilities to the "controllers" of society's future.

It is increasingly evident that man does not believe in man. But God does, and he loves us and knows us through and through. We cannot hide our rottenness from him. Yet, in the face of all our wretched, wavering waywardness, God graciously declares, "My kindness shall not leave you. My promise of peace for you will never be broken...." He said in Ezekiel 33:11: "I have no pleasure in the death of the wicked; I *desire that the wicked turn from his evil ways and live.* Turn, turn from your wickedness, for why will you die...?" Certainly we have the aching heart of the matchless Christ revealed in the words of 2 Peter 3:9: "He is not willing that any should perish,...he is giving more time for sinners to repent."

It does not help a man to brand him. Call him a "scoundrel" and you will probably only incur his hatred. Charge him with crime or cowardice and he will at worst kill you or at best demand proof or recourse according to his code. But, conversely, take him by the hand and say, "Maybe you have fallen deep into sin, but I believe in you still; I have confidence in you; I believe you can recover your lost honor," and the angels of hope will begin to sing again in the prodigal's heart. This is God's attitude toward us. Like a good physician, he does not minimize the reality of disease, and his hatred for that disease is increased only by his love and concern for the patient.

God comes to us as our Lord Jesus Christ came to the woman of Samaria of Jacob's well (John 4). He knew her defilement, her scarlet character, but before he exposed her moral aberration, he revealed that he was her friend. As he sat on the edge of the well he said to the woman whose very touch was moral taint, "Give me to drink." In other words, he was saying to this fallen woman, "I am thirsty and you can refresh me, tired and you can rest me." Regardless of who or what she was, he let her know that she could do something for him. And even as she met his need to the glory of God, so he met hers. He believed in her; he gave her dignity.

What exactly do we mean by the statement, "God believes in us"? First of all, it does not mean that he believes in all that we are. How could he and still be a holy God? Our thoughts are evil and our ways are sinful. We are much of the wickedness upon which God must wage relentless war. Second, it does not mean that he believes in all that we do. How could he and still stand by all his commandments? We do those things we should not do and leave undone those things we should do. God can never overlook the violation of his moral order, because that is the integrity of his existence. Third, it does not mean that God believes in all we profess. Our profession is often better than our practice, but God is not deceived. He is not blind to moral distinctions; he is eternally uncompromising against sin because of what it does in human life. Our hope is not that God has in some way revised the commandments set forth on Mount Sinai, but that, against all that is wrong, there is still found the righteous wrath and condemnation of a holy God. How grateful we should be for this.

If God believes in us, but does not believe in what we *are,* what we *do,* or what we *profess,* then what does he believe in? The answer is that he believes in what we are going to *become.* We are, as it were, in the process of development. We are under construction, and he sees the finished product. He believes not in our fallen, animal, selfish life, but our redeemed, exalted, glorified life—our *future.* He believes that he can more than restore the ruin. We are told in 1 John 3:2, "Dear friends ... we can't imagine what it is going to be like later on. But we do know this, that when he comes we will be like him, as a result of seeing him as he really is."

God sees beyond our disabilities to our possibilities. He does not give us up because we are bad or have failed; this is not and never has been God's way. Israel, for instance, was as wayward as was any people. Her lawgiver was a murderer. The author of her hymnology was an adulterer. Her greatest king wrote the Proverbs likely because he could not keep them. Yet, God believed in the possibilities of the chosen people, and he preserved them until from the Hebrew race came the Savior of the world.

God believes in the ideal rather than that which

is seen in the present. This means that life has a purpose and a fulfillment. A single grain of wheat would be an insufficient breakfast for a sparrow, but when we think of the potential in that single grain, there rises before us the vision of waving fields of golden wheat, enough to satisfy the hunger of the world.

Another way of saying it is that God believes in what we're *becoming.* Consider what he saw in the disciples. Upon meeting Peter our Lord saw *his possibilities* and so he called him a *rock.* Was he a "rock" at that moment? No, but eventually he became one. In time *every one* of his disciples fulfilled his dream for them. When you and I were first thought of it was not the picture of a marred, reprobate life that the great Father carried in his heart. While sin has come between him and his original plan for man, God is pressing on toward its fulfillment, sustained by sublime faith that the soul may one day become as beautiful as it was when he willed it into being. What an answer this is for the millions of people for whom life has no meaning, who cannot in any way authenticate their existence.

Carl Jung recognized the pathetic state of a man without hope when he said that the central neurosis of our time is *emptiness.* Rollo May, the New York psychologist, corroborated Jung's conclusion when he said that on the basis of both his and his colleagues' clinical practice, the chief problem of people in this modern day and age is emptiness. Victor Frankl, who experienced the horror of the Nazi prison camps, wrote a book entitled

Man's Search for Meaning. He said that in order for man to survive he must have some meaning and purpose in life. He related that when a prisoner of war lost faith in the future, he was doomed, for in losing this, he lost his spiritual hold and became subject to mental and physical decay. The loss of hope and courage can have a deadly effect. He concludes that the state of inner emptiness is one of the major challenges to psychiatry today. Obviously, the basic cause of emptiness is a spiritual vacuum. Rob a whole generation of its belief in God, or at least God's purpose for man, and you leave it suspended in mid air—unsupported, unattached, and directionless.

God's faith in the soul's sublime possibility is manifested in all his dealings with men. We see it in that majestic hour when he said, "Let us make man in our image, after our likeness..." (Gen. 1:26). Why launch the human race on its perilous journey if he did not believe in its possibilities, in its future? Why would God give man a revelation if he did not believe in him? Why Calvary? Why the terrible death of the Son of God if God had no faith in man or if man has no future? If he does not believe in man, then why does he strive with him by his Holy Spirit, plead with him in his providences and follow him with a love that all the nights cannot obscure nor all the winters chill?

If you have nothing but your spiritual thirst to commend you, then God believes in you. If you are all ragged and tattered in want, emptiness, loneliness, and purposelessness, then God believes in you. His invitation is to come as you are

150

without money or price. Whoever the man and however far astray or fallen in sin he may be, God can restore him. He can set him on his feet and lift him out of the mire of sin into decency, respectability, peace, joy, and usefulness, up above the stars into the golden glory where he shall see the King in his beauty and become like him. This is vital Christianity, and all who depreciate it do dishonor to the God who created us and the Christ who redeemed us.

The ruined soul can rise! Maybe his friends and his church have lost faith in him; maybe he has even lost faith in himself, but if God still believes in him, he need not despair. Man is saved by faith—not by his faith in himself, nor merely by his faith in God, but primarily by *God's faith in him!* As long as God's strength lasts we need never faint; as long as his hope for man survives we need never falter; as long as his love is ours we can never be poor; as long as he believes in us we may attempt the altar stairs.

Therefore, let us forget our failures and press on. One of the most important skills in life is to be able to forget. It has been said that a man is what he thinks, or what he eats; but a man is also the sum total of what he is able to forget. Memory is one of our greatest faculties. The ability to retain information and experience is of vital importance. But it is a more subtle art to be able to cast out of the mind, or at least from a commanding place in it, all failures and unhappy events that should be forgotten. If a man is to be happy and spiritually effective, he must learn how to forget, to revise

151

the priorities of memory. Too many people today are inhibited, frustrated, and depressed because they are continually haunted by remorse, regret, and memories that bring them only misery.

The best formula for forgetting is found in the Word of God. Philippians 3:13, 14: "This one thing: Forgetting the past and looking forward to what lies ahead, I strain to receive the prize for which God is calling us..." Before his cataclysmic conversion on the Damascus Road, the Apostle Paul's life was one of great sin. It might have so haunted his mind later on that he could have had no ministry.

How do we apply this formula for forgetting? The first step is the simple determination to forget, by turning the matter over to God. We are to turn our backs on what is behind and reach out to that which lies ahead. This is the secret of initiating spiritual growth. We must forget the past with all its faults, sins, mistakes, and sorrows, but we should never forget its lessons. We must "forget" the past in the sense that it brings to our hearts and minds remorse, regret and defeat. It is sad to see, for example, what resentment can do in the life of one who harbors ill will toward another and desires revenge. It inevitably injures his health as well as hampers his powers of logical thinking and ruins any possible effectiveness in the realm of Christian service. When the apostle urges us to "reach forth unto those things which are before, pressing toward the mark of the high calling in Christ Jesus," he is talking about growing up, about spiritual maturity, about a good self-image with the adult pattern in control, about a life totally yielded to the authority and sovereignty of the Holy Spirit.

There are only two things we can do about anything that is past. First, do everything reasonably possible to remedy or repair the situation. Dr. Blanton said that in his opinion, the wisest psychiatric statement ever made was the Apostle Paul's words, "Having done all, stand" (Eph 6:13, KJV). Therapy is based on the simple process of doing all we can, the best we can, and then realizing there is nothing further we can do. There is no point in fretting, worrying, engaging in mental postmortems, or rehashing the situation. We have done all we can do; therefore, we must stand.

Second, we must totally commit the matter to God. We should conceive of it as lying in the past, growing ever more dim against the horizon as each day carries us farther away from it.

We vindicate God's faith in us when we realize the hidden possibilities within us. But before this can happen, we must know exactly what we are. One of the most meaningful phrases in the story of the Prodigal Son is found in the words, "When he finally came to his senses" (Luke 15:17). This was his moment of self-discovery; he realized in a flash who he was, where he was, and that he was on the wrong track. He seemed to say to himself, "Why am I wallowing with pigs when I can live with my father?" The Word of God says he determined, "I will go home to my father..." (vs. 18). When he saw himself as he actually was, he decided to become the man God meant him to be.

153

God cannot help us unless we honestly see ourselves as God sees us. Sometimes this is a painful operation because we are prone to self-deception. But from that moment of absolute honesty before God, life moves onward and upward; it becomes aggressive, radiant, victorious. Dr. Thomas Harris said that as long as people are bound to the past, they are not free to be themselves or to respond to the needs and hopes of others. William Durant said that to say we are free merely means that we know what we are doing, which to me is one of the best explanations of our Lord's words in John 8:36: "So if the Son sets you free, you will indeed be free."

One of the most profound truths ever set down for man's guidance is the well-known phrase, "As a man thinketh in his heart, so is he" (Prov. 23:7, KJV). This Scripture expresses deep insight into human nature and what is known as *projected image therapy.* In the last analysis, a man is what he has been predominantly sending into the controlling center of his life. The ideas or thoughts that finally determine our actions and character are not those we receive and examine in the conscious mind. The conscious mind is only a receiving station, a "reception office" where thoughts—good, bad, and innocuous—are examined and passed on. Some are rejected and have little opportunity to have any effect. But the thoughts, good or bad, that are received hospitably, repeatedly, and with welcome eventually become the thoughts a man "thinketh in his heart" and presently "so is."

No matter how sordid or evil a thought may be,

when it first enters a mind it does not touch the personality with its infamy or in any way lay guilt upon the soul unless and until the mind, acting as a judge, admits it with a welcome. If the mind decides against it and dismisses it, the personality is not only unsullied, but is stimulated and strengthened in moral and spiritual power. If the thought is welcomed, it is as though all its evil implications have been actualized. Jesus emphasized this when he said, "Anyone who even looks at a woman with lust in his eye has already committed adultery with her in his heart" (Matt. 5:28). This does not imply a passing, unadmitted, impure thought, but a definitely entertained desire.

To illustrate this, if I am very hungry and I walk past a window where there is a barbecue spit and something luscious and juicy roasting on it, and I stand, looking in the window, watching it turn, I have absolutely no power over my salivary glands. All of a sudden my mouth starts to water and the gastric juices begin to flow into my stomach because my body doesn't know any law but the gratification and satisfaction of its own desires. If I think, "I haven't the money," and go on my way, I have done nothing wrong. But if I stand there and think, "If there were only some way I could get someone to distract the chef so I could get a knife and whack off a hunk of that meat, I would do it!" and I begin to connive, Jesus said that I might as well have committed the act.

Before every deed there is a thought, or a succession of thoughts. Before the thief ever steals with his hand he steals with his mind. Before the immoral act is performed the mind has already committed the offense. If the thought of a wrong act has never been favorably entertained by the mind, the act itself will never take place. The issue is determined not at the moment of crisis by rational and objective thinking, but by the resistance or lack of it in the subconscious mind or soul, a resistance that has been strengthened or weakened each time the conscious mind rejects or accepts a thought.

What we really are, then, is based on how we program ourselves, and this determines the inevitable playback. When we pour into our minds and hearts the truths of the Word of God and are prayerfully obedient to the Spirit of God, unconsciously our character is determined. You can get out of a computer only what you put into it. And what we have put into our lives—that is, what we feed upon—at last determines what we are and what comes out of us. The tapes will only replay the recorded information. It has been said that we should be careful what we wish because t is what we may become. The mask will someday slip from the face, and the truth will out.

In each of us lie hidden possibilities or energies which can defeat us if not understood and properly used, but which can endow us with great power for successful and effective living if wisely used by God. When these energies are brought under the influence of Jesus Christ, the most amazing results appear in people whose lives were formerly commonplace or defeated. When men

156

and women accept Jesus Christ as the Lord of their lives, it is a surrender of self to God by an act of faith and a wholehearted desire to follow God's will. This spiritual experience causes us to become what God means us to be, and it goes deeper into the personality; it lays a controlling hand upon the unconscious mind or soul, the inner life force, and holds firmly in check destructive elements and releases hidden energies that produce a person of spiritual adequacy.

A young businessman in his late thirties told of the following experience. He was brought up in a devout Christian home, but like many others he drifted away from his spiritual heritage. After marriage he became deeply engrossed in his business, and attended church only once a year. Increasingly the emphasis of his life was materialistic and secular; he lived for the accumulation of things that money could buy. Suddenly, his business failed and he became a victim of unrelieved depression. Then he encountered a radiant personality who seemed to possess a depth of peace and confidence in dramatic contrast to his own unrest and despair. He asked the secret and the answer was the reality of Jesus Christ in his life.

He responded, "Why, I believe in Christ."

Said his friend, "That may be true, but have you ever absolutely and completely placed yourself in his hands?"

He admitted that his belief was evidently nothing more than intellectual acceptance and confidence in biblical truth and in the identity of Jesus Christ. Then came that moment when he cast himself upon the mercy of Christ and embraced him as Lord and Savior in a total, unconditional commitment. Live wires tapped his personality as the days went by, and the deeper he mined in the Word of God the more he found a spiritual transformation taking place. He made an interesting statement: "All my life I've been more or less around Christianity, but it always seemed a rather dead thing to me. Strange how different it is now. But one thing is sure: when you actually take it into your life spiritually, it does everything it says it will!"

God believes in us! So let us learn a lesson from our failures and then forget them. Let us realize the hidden possibilities within us by seeing to it that our yielding to Jesus Christ is not fragmentary, but total. Allow the Spirit of God to take over your life in such a way that all your thought processes, all you are, and have, and ever hope to be, belong to him.

"When someone becomes a Christian he becomes a brand new person inside. He is not the same any more. A new life has begun! All these new things are from God who brought us back to himself through what Christ Jesus did. And God has given us the privilege of urging everyone to come into his favor and be reconciled to him" (2 Cor. 5:17, 18).

◆ ◆ ◆

When someone becomes a Christian
he becomes a brand new person inside. He is not the
same any more. A new life has begun.
2 CORINTHIANS 5:17